SPITFIRE

Text by Bill Sweetman

Illustrations by Rikyu Watanabe

Crown Publishers, Inc.

New York

Spitfire control column head with
oamera switch and (Va model only)
gunfiring button.

Spitfire MX IID Gyro gun sight

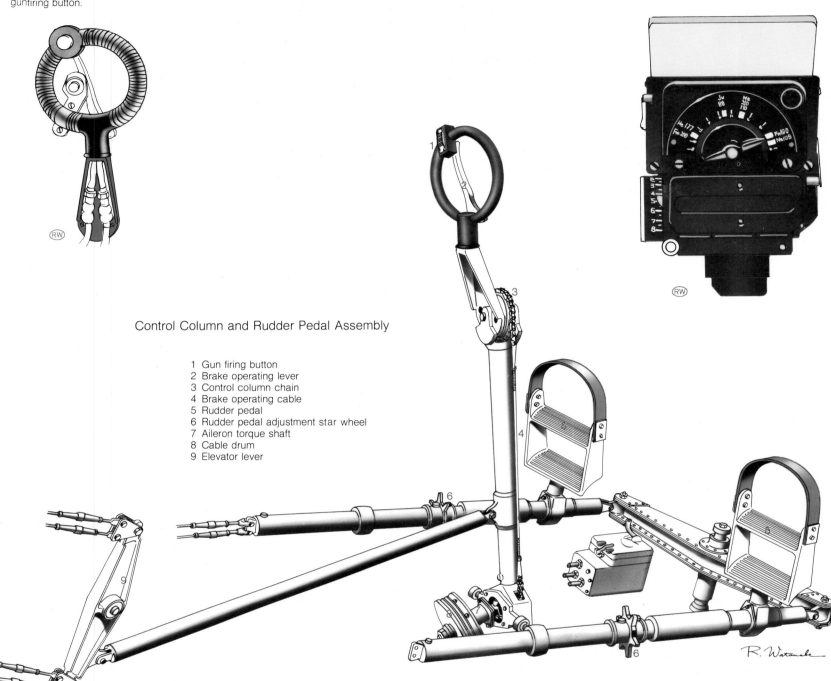

Control Column and Rudder Pedal Assembly

1 Gun firing button
2 Brake operating lever
3 Control column chain
4 Brake operating cable
5 Rudder pedal
6 Rudder pedal adjustment star wheel
7 Aileron torque shaft
8 Cable drum
9 Elevator lever

R. Watanabe

This book was designed and produced by Wing & Anchor Press,
a division of Zokeisha Publications, Ltd.,
5-1-6, Roppongi, Minato-ku, Tokyo/123 East 54th Street, New York, N.Y. 10022.

©1980 by Zokeisha Publications, Ltd.

First published in the U.S.A. by Crown Publishers, Inc.,
One Park Avenue, New York, N.Y. 10016.

Printed and bound in Japan.
First printing, August, 1980.

ISBN No. 0-517-542617
Library of Congress Catalog Card Number: 80-23763

Something about a Spitfire

There are few of mankind's artifacts which have stood for so much in the consciousness of an entire nation as the Spitfire. Those to whom the Spitfire is part of history—and this number includes the author—can experience only at second-hand the identification of the graceful shape of the Supermarine fighter with that 'finest hour' of tension and conflict—yet it was of that identification that the legend was made.

The fact that the Hurricane—the dashing Spitfire's trusty but unimaginative esquire—bore by far the greatest weight of the Battle of Britain, and that without the sturdy and easily built Hawker fighter the control of the air over Southern England would have been lost, seem to count for nothing. The Hurricane was just never photogenic; it looked like a monoplane which had not quite shrugged off the chrysalis of the biplane. But neither are the inevitable deficiencies of the Spitfire taken into account in the formation of the legend: it was a production engineer's nightmare, a torment for the armourer and a tricky and weak-kneed carrier fighter. This is not to denigrate the design, but to view it as simply one more military aircraft.

But there is one respect in which the Spitfire and Seafire are equalled by no other aircraft in history: development. The Spitfire was one of the first all-metal, low-wing, retractable-undercarriage, enclosed-canopy monoplane fighters, but it was also one of the last to remain in production, only the Sea Fury and Corsair (both of much later design) outlasting it. In the eleven years between the delivery of the first Spitfire I and the completion of the last Seafire FR.47, a constant and dynamic development process, ever flexible and always ready to incorporate the latest technology, had kept the fighter fully competitive with its contemporaries.

The Spitfire was conceived when the importance of speed and rate of climb was beginning to be recognised. Turning performance had been sacrificed to some extent with the demise of the biplane, while forward and downward vision was traded off against lower drag with the move from the Supermarine 224, built for the F.7/30 contest, to the Type 300 Spitfire. However, what had not been foreseen was the extent to which success in combat was to depend on the advantages of momentum and surprise, calling as never before on speed and rate of climb to give the fighter leader the option of giving or refusing combat. Of equal importance was the firepower to deal out a lethal burst before concentration on the target proved fatal.

It was in the crucial aspects of speed, rate of climb and firepower that the Spitfire was developed as no other aircraft has been. Compare the mighty FR.47 with the dainty Spitfire I: Top speed, 25 per cent greater; time to 20,000 ft (6,100 m), 49 per cent less; weight of fire per second, trebled. The increased performance meant more power, a hefty 128 per cent more in point of fact, delivered through a massive six-blade contraprop instead of a two-blade fixed-pitch airscrew. Part of the 111 per cent weight increase was accounted for by 81 per cent more fuel to slake the thirst of the Griffon engine; part by the heavier armament; another slice by the 80 per cent heavier powerplant, and the rest by the extra stainless steel and aluminum required to make the thing hang together. All in all, the resulting Seafire FR.47 had barely a component in common with the Spitfire I, but retained the general arrangement and the balance of flying qualities which had characterised the original.

Development of the Spitfire was the result of two factors: the massive increase in power made available from a package of broadly similar dimensions—and, particularly, similar cross-sectional area—and the ability of the airframe to absorb such power. The former was the product of the intense development efforts which Rolls-Royce placed on the design of mechanical supercharging systems from the late 1920s, allowing the increase of power without increase in cross-section area. An equally important engine development was the design of the Griffon engine to offer 36 per cent more capacity in a package the same size as a Merlin.

The ability of the airframe to take such power, however, is barely comprehensible. It stemmed from the fact that the wing was both large enough in area to support the consequent weight growth and thin enough in section to avoid the problems of 'compressibility' which would have cropped up with a thicker wing as fighting speeds increased. The risk inherent in designing such a wing is that it will be either excessively heavy or insufficiently rigid, but the wing of the Spitfire was designed in such a way that it avoided both risks. Admittedly, a lack of torsional rigidity in the wing affected the Spitfire's ability to roll in a high-speed dive, at least until the Mark 21 appeared, but in the test of combat this defect was never proved crucial until the late stages of the war.

It was the great span of the Spitfire's wing which endowed it with lower induced drag—air resistance related to lift—than its contemporaries, while the thin section freed it from the profile drag which limited the Hurricane. Its aerodynamic efficiency was therefore outstanding, particularly at the high altitudes and relatively low air speeds where induced drag becomes of greatest importance. Hence the Spitfire's outstanding turning performance at low airspeeds, and the ease with which it was adapted as a high-altitude strategic reconnaissance aircraft.

One can only wonder how much R.J. Mitchell foresaw of the future development of the little fighter which he watched on its maiden flight in March, 1936. Mitchell himself had little more than a year to live; and the design of the Spitfire was redolent of second sight, the last inspired work of a dying artist.

Creation of a Legend

There must be as many legends surrounding the story of the Supermarine Type 300 Spitfire and its many descendants as there were examples of the aircraft itself. This is a pity, because the facts are themselves remarkable enough. What distinguishes the Spitfire from almost all other aircraft which can be accurately described as 'classic' is that neither its forbears nor its descendants can make any claim whatsoever to that status. The quality of the Spitfire, both in its basic design and its prodigious capacity for development, was apparently an unrepeatable combination of elements, a classic case of the whole being greater than the sum of its parts. Had you told a seasoned aviation observer in 1930 that the next generation of fighting aircraft for the Royal Air Force would be predominantly of Supermarine design, he would have nodded and smiled politely; if you had told the same man in 1945 that within two generations of aircraft the Supermarine name would have vanished completely, he would probably have considered you insane. However, that is exactly what did happen: the name of Supermarine came and went, leaving the world's most famous aircraft as its memorial.

The name itself was coined in September, 1913, when it was adopted as the telegraphic address of a small aircraft factory on a Southampton wharf. Its founder, Noel Pemberton-Billing, was an enthusiastic aviator and designer of indifferent marine aircraft, some of which were distinguished by removable wings without which the hull was intended to function as a cabin cruiser. In 1917, after a career with the Royal Naval Air Service, Pemberton-Billing entered Parliament and on one occasion was expelled from the chamber when his expostulations against the unprepared state of the British air defences grew too extreme.

The factory he founded, which in a later conflict was to be synonymous with those defences, was by this time in other hands. Headed by Hugh Scott-Paine, the Supermarine Aviation Works had in 1916 employed a 21-year-old engineer from the Midlands, named Reginald J. Mitchell. Within three years he was the company's chief designer: a high-sounding position, but less secure than it might have been given the state of British aviation at the time. Post-war cuts in military expenditure had hit the emerging Royal Air Force heavily—the Cinderella service's two older and uglier sisters had more political muscle and no interest in a third independent service—and the consequent sales of redundant military aircraft reduced the market for new commercial aircraft to virtually zero. However, the company continued to produce small marine aircraft sharing a similar basic layout: biplane wings with the engine between them, above the hull. Not only was this basic layout visible in service for the next 20 years, in the comfortingly sturdy shape of the Walrus rescue and reconnaissance amphibian, but despite its apparent lack of aerodynamic qualities it succeeded in winning races, bringing the Schneider Trophy back to Britain in 1922.

By that time, however, the Schneider Trophy seaplane race was on its way to becoming a contest of international machismo on a grand scale. The races of the 1923 and subsequent years would see a strong field of much more modern competitors, with speeds rising from the 145 mph (233 km/h) of the 1922 winner to well above 200 mph (320 km/h). Mitchell and his team—which now included another young Midlander, Joe Smith—set to work on a radical new machine which would beat even the US navy's purpose-built Curtiss racers.

After a brief flirtation with a flying-boat design in which the propeller was to be driven via shafts and gearing from an engine buried in the hull, R.J. Mitchell drew up the

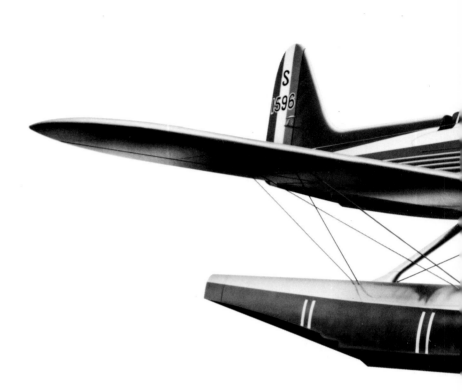

Supermarine S6B (S1695), winner of the final 1931 Schneider Trophy race at an average speed of 340.08 mph (547.29 km/h). This and the subsequent new speed record of 408.8 mph (657.88 km/h) were achieved thanks to very careful streamlining combined with (for those days) high wing loading and the light water-cooled Rolls-Royce R engine developing 2300 hp at only 1630 lb (739.4 kg) weight.

design of a seaplane called the S.4. The new floatplane was flown for the first time in August, 1925, a mere five months after receipt of an Air Ministry contract to develop a high-speed seaplane 'for research purposes.' The most revolutionary feature of the S.4 was its unbraced (cantilever) monoplane wing, and this may also have been its weakest point. After setting a new world air speed record, the S.4 crashed in practice over the 1925 Schneider course at Baltimore. Not enough of the thin plywood wing was fished from the harbour to permit the cause of the accident to be determined, but Mitchell's later seaplanes reverted to streamlined bracing wires on their wings. They also had all-metal fuselages instead of the wooden structure of the S.4.

In the 1927 race at Venice, Mitchell's less lovely but sturdier S.5 took the first of three successive victories for the British Government team. The S.5, like the S.4, was powered by a Napier Lion engine with a 'broad arrow' configuration, having three banks of four cylinders converging from above on a single crankshaft. The US victors of the 1923 race at Cowes, however, had sparked off a chain of events that was to provide a powerplant not only for the last and fastest of the Supermarine racers, but also for their more warlike descendants.

British aircraft manufacturer C.R. Fairey had been among the spectators in 1923 as Lt. David Rittenhouse raced the Curtiss CR-3 to victory. He was more impressed, however, by the racer's powerplant, a narrow-angle V-12 engine of 'monobloc' construction—the cylinders were cast into a solid block rather than comprising separate liners and cooling jackets. Arthur Nutt's Curtiss D-12 offered a tremendous

R. Watanabe

advantage in streamlining over the bulky wartime engines then in service. A month after the race, Fairey had agreed with Curtiss to import a batch of D-12s, with an option on licence production, and had started the design of a light bomber based on the American engine.

The speed performance of the resulting Fairey Fox was sensational, but its impact was hardly what Fairey had anticipated. The Air Ministry remained profoundly uninterested in buying large quantities of Foxes powered by Curtiss-Fairey engines, and instead dispatched a D-12 (called the Felix in Britain) to Rolls-Royce. The august British company dropped its first postwar development, the powerful but complex Eagle 16, and produced a narrow-angle V-12. At first referred to as the Falcon X, the engine later became known as the Rolls-Royce F before being finally christened the Kestrel, and it was Kestrel-powered, Hawker-built Harts rather than Foxes which became the RAF's fastest light bombers.

It was a call to patriotism that persuaded Rolls-Royce to convert its scaled-up Kestrel, the 36.7-litre Buzzard, into a racing engine for Mitchell's 1929 Schneider contender, the S.6. (Racing was, of course, anathema to the utterly conservative Derby company.) The ingredient which Rolls-Royce added to the basic V-12 engine to produce the R racing powerplant was a massive mechanically driven supercharger, with a centrifugal rotor tailored to the S.6 fuselage. The advantages of supercharging were many; above all, the compression of the air before induction into the engine increased the power output without the increase in weight and frontal area which would have been incurred had

the engine simply been scaled up. The supercharger was moreover fed by a ram inlet, gaining extra compression and power virtually as a free by-product of the aircraft's forward speed.

By 1931, when the ultimate S.6B set a world's air speed record at 407 mph (655 km/hr), the R engine was generating 2,530 hp. This was a long way from a service rating; after every full-power run, the engine had to be stripped and overhauled, and its consumption of a specially developed cocktail of benzol, methanol, acetone and lead was phenomenal. As well as pioneering the use of high supercharger boost ratios, the R was the first Rolls-Royce engine to feature high-strength aluminum forgings and sodium-cooled valves.

At that time Rolls-Royce's military hopes largely rested on the Goshawk, an engine closely related to the Kestrel but featuring a novel system of cooling in which the water was allowed to boil and was then condensed into steam in pressurised surface radiators. This powerplant was embodied in several of the designs being prepared to meet Air Ministry specification F.7/30, which called for a new 250 mph fighter for the RAF.

One of the designs was from Supermarine, which had been taken over by armaments giant Vickers-Armstrong in 1928. (Vickers had its own aviation division, which remained in business separately and produced the Jockey fighter to F.7/30.) However, neither Supermarine nor Vickers nor Rolls-Royce emerged victorious from the F.7/30 competition, since the conservative evolutionary design of the Bristol-powered Gloster Gauntlet biplane turned out to meet what had been regarded as revolutionary specifications. For Supermarine and Rolls-Royce, it was time to adopt a policy of *reculer pour mieux sauter*.

Flown in February, 1934, the Supermarine F.7/30 or Type 224 was a mix of old and new. The wing was of cantilever design, but the type featured a fixed undercarriage and a fixed-pitch propeller and lacked landing flaps. Retractable gear, variable-pitch propellers and split flaps had been demonstrated on the American Douglas DC-1 airliner in the previous year, and the airframe of the 224 was similar in its technology level to that of the Boeing P-26 of 1932. Flight-testing of the Goshawk in the 224 and other F.7/30 contenders was also to prove that steam-cooling (or surface evaporation cooling) was not a practical proposition for combat aircraft. A beneficial result of this failure was that the British industry avoided the long flirtation with zero-drag evaporative cooling which was to plague many German aircraft programmes.

In any event, developments in aviation between the issue of F.7/30 and the appearance of the prototypes designed to meet it had rendered the specification obsolete. The appearance of the Heinkel He70 Blitz light transport in late 1932 had confirmed that Germany was not far behind the United States in airframe technology. F.7/30 had been founded on the premise that higher speeds would be needed if aircraft comparable to the Hart were to be intercepted successfully; only something altogether more potent would suffice if an enemy was to introduce a bomber based on the 1933 technology of the Blitz or the DC-1. It was also becoming accepted that the tight-turning dogfight of the 1914-18 war was no longer the

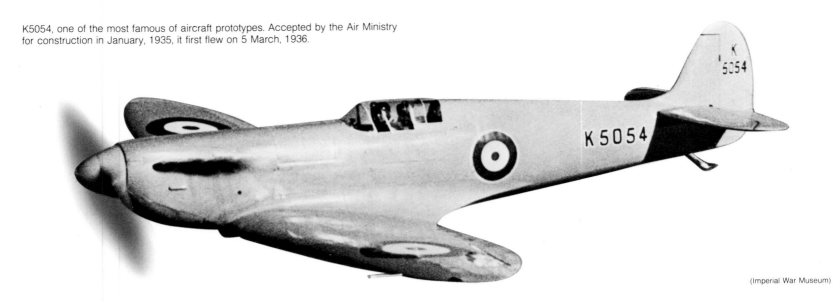

K5054, one of the most famous of aircraft prototypes. Accepted by the Air Ministry for construction in January, 1935, it first flew on 5 March, 1936.

(Imperial War Museum)

best way to prevent an escorted bomber force from reaching its target; speed to overhaul an enemy aircraft, and firepower to destroy it in a single burst, became the targets of the aircraft industry.

The Royal Air Force, responsible for drawing up specifications for such aircraft, had survived the savage blows of the immediate post-war era, and in 1923 won the significant victory of parity in authority with the Army and Navy. Under Stanley Baldwin's administration some sort of air-defence force and organisation had been created. In the absence of any device for giving advance warning of the approach of enemy bombers, however, defence against air attack was regarded as of low priority. Fighter development advanced hardly at all between 1920 and 1930, and production of the Fury was curtailed in favour of the cheaper but slower Bulldog. Defence spending in general was governed by the 'ten-year-rule,' which laid down that hostilities in Europe would be heralded by ten years of increasing tension. This policy ceased to carry weight from 1930 onwards, and, although the Air Estimates remained constant through 1932-34, spending virtually trebled over the next two years and rose by another 50 per cent in 1936-38. The years of 1934-36 were not unnaturally a period of great fertility in new technical ideas.

As often happens in the development of aircraft, it was the engine manufacturer which made the first move. By 1932, possibly in anticipation of trouble with the Goshawk, Rolls-Royce was working on an engine 20 per cent bigger than the Kestrel but using some of the racing engines' technology to yield an output similar to that of the much larger Buzzard. Initially, Rolls-Royce proposed that the engine should be inverted to allow the pilot a better view over the nose, but manufacturers reactions to this unfamiliar arrangement were negative. Accordingly, it was an upright V-12 engine which made its first run in November, 1933. Known as the PV-12, it was later to join the other birds of prey in the company aviary as the Merlin.

The Merlin was designed to yield about 1,000 hp for combat, in its initial service version. The ratio of supercharger speed to crankshaft speed was fixed. In consequence the speed of the supercharger could not be adjusted to cope with variations in atmospheric pressure at various altitudes.

The engine thus had to be throttled back to prevent excess pressure, detonation and damage below the altitude at which the supercharger and engine were best matched: the 'rated altitude' at which the engine would give its best power. This 'tuning' of the engine to the role performed by any particular variant of the aircraft was a highly important factor in the versatility of the aircraft powered by the Merlin.

Another element of the Spitfire's design originated in 1933, when the Armament Research Department of the Air Ministry organised a design competition to find a replacement for the Vickers machine-gun. The 1914-18-vintage Vickers was so prone to jam that it had to be located within the pilot's reach. It hence fired through the airscrew disc, incurring penalties in rate of fire and the complexity of a mechanical synchronising system. The American 0.300-in Colt was selected from a field of six weapons as the best basis for a replacement and was put into production as the Browning, firing standard British 0.303-in ammunition.

By early 1934, the Air Ministry was looking for a new fighter to carry these weapons, and was suggesting that it should be ten per cent faster than the Gladiator (a refined version of the F.7/30-winning Gauntlet). Hawker responded with a monoplane incorporating several features of the Fury, while Supermarine's proposal was a refined extrapolation of the disappointing 224 featuring a retractable undercarriage, enclosed cockpit and split flaps on a smaller wing. Both were offered with the Goshawk until late 1934, when steam-cooling was abandoned in favour of the new PV-12, and were armed with four wing-mounted machine guns. At the beginning of 1935 the manufacturers received specification F.37/34, written around their new aircraft, and in the course of the year the Air Ministry decided to investigate the possibility of installing no fewer than eight of the new machine guns to give greater lethality against the new twin-engined bombers then under development in Germany. This requirement, set out in specification F.10/35, suggested that the eight guns might be made movable in some way; armament policy was not irrevocably committed to the use of eight machine guns, and in late 1934 the rival concept of the two-seat turret fighter was being pursued in parallel with the Supermarine and Hawker fixed-gun studies.

Throughout 1935 R.J. Mitchell led his team in the

creation of the Supermarine Type 300, probably aware that he might never live to see it fly; he had fallen victim in 1933 to the cancer which was to kill him four years later. Joe Smith later recalled the chief designer's technique: 'He would modify the lines of an aircraft with the softest pencil he could find, and then remodel over the top with progressively thicker lines, until one would finally be faced with a new outline of lines about 3/16ths of an inch thick. But the results were usually worthwhile and the centre of the line was usually accepted when the thing was redrawn.' In this way the shape of the Spitfire emerged from the chrysalis of the 224. To begin with, the 224 fuselage could be modified in light of the relaxation of requirements on forward view in favour of greater speed. The fuselage of the new aircraft was faired neatly from the PV-12 engine and supercharger, flowing past the tightly hooded cockpit in unbroken straight lines to the tail in the original manner of the S.4 and its successors.

The wing was the unique feature which was to distinguish the Spitfire from all its contemporaries and endow it with most of its outstanding qualities. That the elliptical wing shape represented something close to an ideal had been acknowledged for some years. It combined the long span needed for aerodynamic efficiency at high altitudes with some of the structural attributes of a short-span wing, because so much of its area was carried well inboard. The comparatively long chord of the wing roots meant that the landing gear and (in early 1935) four-gun armament of the Type 300 could be buried completely within a wing of low thickness-to-chord ratio and correspondingly low drag. (After the unhappy experience with the thick wing of the 224, this consideration must have weighed heavily on Mitchell's mind.) Eventually, the Type 300 emerged with a wing section thinner than any other fighter of its day, and this was probably the most important factor in the extraordinary potential for development which it was to display over the next ten years.

The structure of the wing was unique, and in part a legacy from the 224. The steam-cooling system of the Goshawk engine demanded that the entire leading edge of the wing be devoted to condensers, and to this end the leading edge forward of the single mainspar was sealed and formed into a structural torsion box. This technique was refined on

the 300 to provide sufficient stiffness and strength in the thin, large-area wing. The mainspar itself was formed of square-section tubes 'telescoped' together so that the narrowest and longest extended to the tip of the wing; the number of concentric tubes forming the spar decreased from root to tip. The spar was close to the structural ideal, being tapered in fore-and-aft and up-and-down axes, and nowhere thicker than it had to be. The spar could also be fairly readily 'beefed up' in development by extending the inner tube sections. The wing ribs forward of the spar and the heavy-gauge skin of the leading edge formed the rest of the torsion box that gave the wing its strength and light weight. Later in the development of the Spitfire it was found how exactly R.J. Mitchell and Joe Smith had tailored the strength of the wing to the job which it had to do.

The Spitfire was to take advantage of two other innovations before it reached the RAF squadrons. Possibly the most important was the ducted radiator developed at the Royal Aircraft Establishment, Farnborough, which considerably reduced the extra drag incurred with the replacement of the surface-evaporation-cooled Goshawk by the PV-12. Instead of being simply thrust out into the airflow, the radiator was housed in an aerodynamic duct which was designed so that some of the heat shed by the radiator was recovered in the form of thrust as the heated air escaped from the duct. Another new feature, similarly offering a benefit from otherwise wasted energy, was the ejector exhaust nozzle, which simply directed the energy of the escaping exhaust rearwards. The extra power was worth about 70 hp at 300 mph.

The move to an eight-gun armament in the course of 1935 reduced the new fighter's fuel capacity, which in any event was based on home-defence requirements. From the initially specified 94 Imp gal (427 lit), adequate for two hours at cruise power and half an hour's combat, capacity was reduced to 85 Imp gal (378 lit) enough for 1.65 hours cruising and 15 minutes combat. Range and endurance were never improved to the point where the Spitfire could be compared with later fighter aircraft, although some of the breed were, paradoxically, among the longest-ranged single-engined aircraft of the war years.

At the time of the new type's first flight from

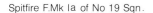
Spitfire F.Mk Ia of No 19 Sqn.

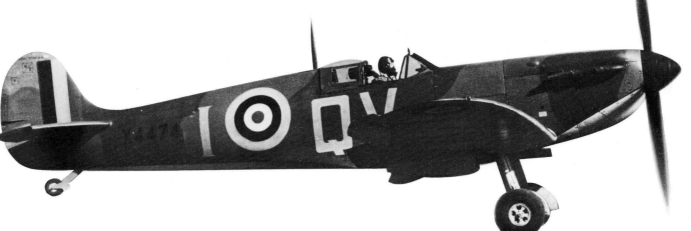

(Imperial War Museum)

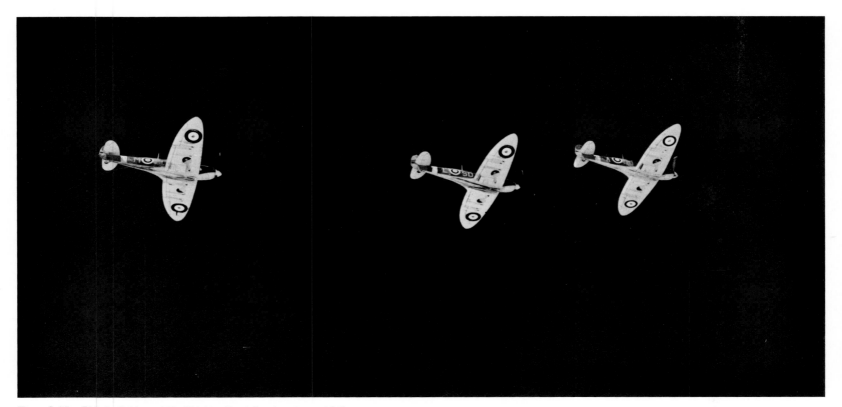

Three Spitfire F.Mk Ia fighters of No 501 (Auxiliary) Sqn in autumn, 1940.

Southampton's Eastleigh airport on 6 March, 1936, it was still referred to in public as the F.37/34; by July of that year the name 'Spitfire' had been officially adopted, but is not clear at what point the aircraft had been christened. The new aircraft changed little during its flight tests, beyond the addition of the newly developed ejector exhausts, camouflage and armament. It was rapidly realized that it was both faster and more manoeuvrable than its Hawker contemporary, by then named Hurricane, and in June, 1936, the Air Ministry ordered 310 Spitfire Is.

The first Spitfire production order formed part of Scheme F, the latest of a series of expansion plans for the RAF; the very first had appeared in mid-1934 as developments in Europe became perceptibly more threatening. Scheme F was the first to include modern fighters, but although earlier schemes were to be criticised as encouraging the production of obsolescent aircraft, they had been invaluable in building up a trained workforce before the new designs were ready to be put into production. In addition, facilities used for cars and commercial vehicles in peacetime were designated as 'shadow factories' for the construction of military aircraft. The Spitfire was due to be built at the Nuffield factory at Castle Bromwich.

Scheme F called for 310 Spitfires to be delivered by March, 1939, but the program soon slipped behind schedule. There were two basic reasons for this. The first, which also affected the Hurricane, was the delayed development of the Merlin engine. In March, 1937, the prototype Spitfire belly-landed after a connecting rod failed. The original Merlin C had failed its 100-hour type test in the month the Spitfire flew, while the initial production Merlin (Merlin F or Merlin I) only passed its type test with a limitation on valve life in November, 1936. It was decided to apply this engine to the Fairey Battle bomber and fit the new fighters with the improved Merlin II, and this understandably caused some delay.

The other problem was confined to the Spitfire. Whereas the Hurricane was structurally still closely related to its ancestor the Fury, the Spitfire introduced stressed-skin construction throughout (apart from fabric-covered control surfaces). New techniques had to be devised to mass-produce the new fighter's sophisticated airframe, the Pressed Steel Company's work on the production of the complicated mainspar being particularly noteworthy. However, by September, 1939 only 306 Spitfires had been delivered, six months after the scheduled handover date for the last of the initial 310-aircraft order. By that time, however, production of the Hurricane and Spitfire—together, it is easily forgotten, with that of the misconceived Defiant—was in full swing.

A number of changes were either introduced in the production of the Spitfire I or incorporated during the early production stages. After early service experience the flat-topped cockpit canopy, which tall pilots had found a little restrictive, was replaced with the characteristic bulged hood from the Malcolm Company. A fixed tailwheel replaced the prototype's skid. A more significant change came about from the 78th aircraft, which was the first to boast a three-blade metal two-pitch propeller made by de Havilland. From the 175th aircraft the Merlin III was standardised, this engine being modified to yield about 10 per cent more power than the Merlin II at a slightly lower altitude.

The manually controlled two-pitch airscrew was a considerable advance, reducing the take-off run by 30 per cent and increasing the speed of fastest climb from 175 mph (281 km/hr) to 192 mph (310 km/hr). However, it created another problem for the pilot: it was all to easy to forget, and the propeller was a poor substitute for a genuine constant-speed unit which would automatically adjust the pitch of the blades to the speed of the aircraft.

This, then, was the standard Spitfire at the outbreak of war, after the ironing out of remarkably few prob-

Spitfire Mk Vb

Armour protection

1 Front of header tank
2 Ammunition boxes
3 Front of fuel tank
4 Top of fuel tank
  (cowling panel)

5 Windscreen
6 Pilot's head
7 Back of pilot's seat
8 Bottom of pilot's seat

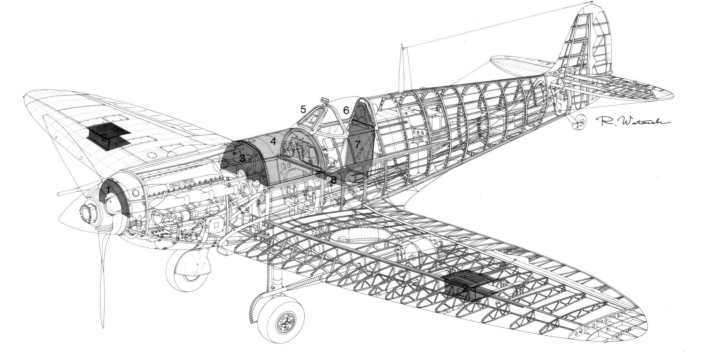

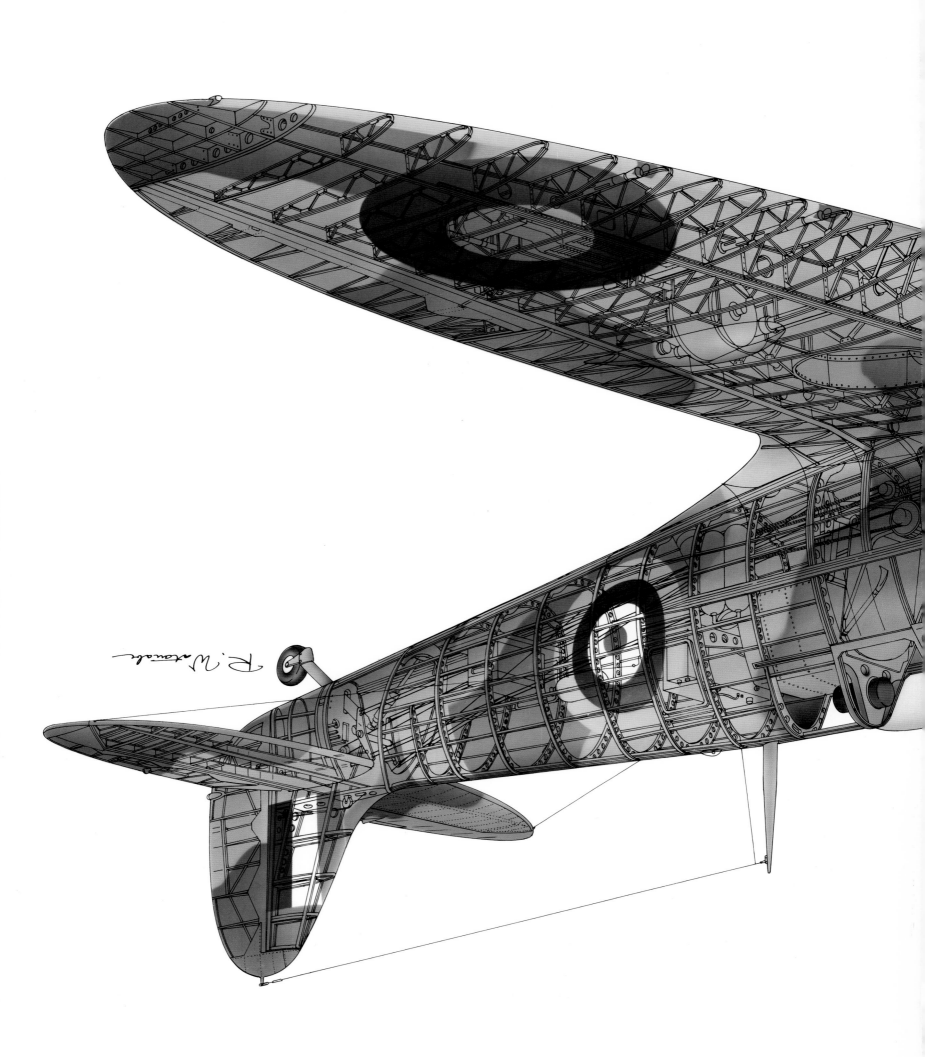

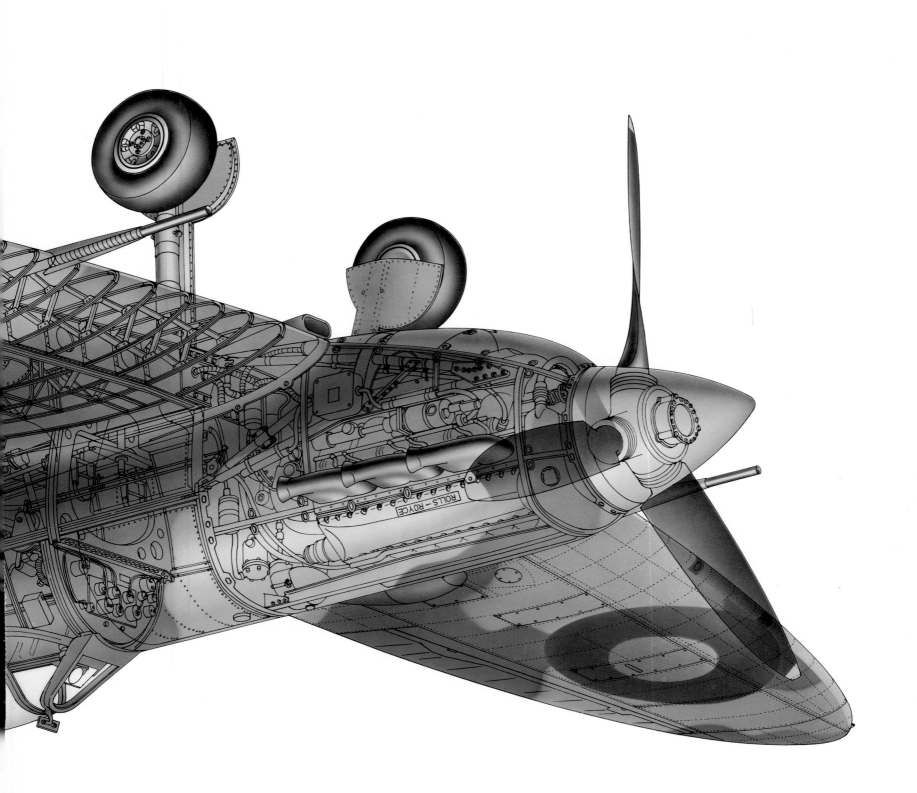

Supermarine Spitfire Vb Cutaway

1 Spinner
2 Propeller hub
3 Rotol, R.X. 5/10 35°pitch range three-blade constant-speed propeller
4 Glycol header tank
5 Rolls-Royce Merlin 45 engine
6 'Fishtail' exhaust manifold
7 Generator
8 Exposed oil tank
9 Hydraulic tank
10 Firewall
11 Oil filter
12 Fuel filter
13 Oil pipe
14 Main engine support member
15 Engine bearer attachment
16 Main fuselage fuel tank (48 gal/218 ltr)
17 Instrument panel
18 Rudder pedals
19 Rudder bar
20 King post
21 Fuselage lower fuel tank (37 gal/168 ltr)
22 Rear-view mirror
23 Reflector gunsight
24 Armoured windscreen
25 Plexiglass canopy
26 Headrest
27 Structural bulkhead
28 Radio controller
29 Pilot's seat

30 Engine control lever
31 Elevator trim controller
32 Rudder tab controller
33 Control column
34 Voltage regulator
35 Cockpit aft glazing
36 Canopy track
37 Auxiliary long-range fuel tank (29 gal/132 ltr)
38 Datum longeron
39 Air bottles (alternative rear fuselage stowage)
40 Aerial mast
41 Aerial lead-in
42 HF aerial
43 Dorsal formation light
44 Radio compartment
45 Access door
46 Backbone longeron
47 Rear oxygen bottle
48 Battery compartment
49 Lower longeron
50 Tailwheel oleo shock-absorber
51 Fuselage angled frame
52 Elevator control lever
53 Rudder control lever
54 Cross shaft
55 Fuselage double frame
56 Tailwheel strut
57 Castoring non-retractable tailwheel
58 Aerial stub attachment
59 Fabric-covered rudder
60 Rudder tab
61 Rudder tab hinge
62 Sternpost

63 Fin rear spar (fuselage frame extension)
64 Fin front spar (fuselage frame extension)
65 Tailplane front spar
66 Port tailplane
67 Port elevator
68 Elevator tab
69 Rear navigation light
70 IFF aerial
71 Port navigation light
72 Wingtip structure
73 Port aileron construction
74 Aileron hinge
75 Bellcrank
76 Aileron push tube
77 Machine-gun support brackets
78 0.303-in machine-gun, with 350 rounds of ammunition
79 Ammunition boxes (350 rpg)
80 Cannon magazine drum (120 rounds)
81 Aileron control cables
82 Flap structure
83 Mainwheel well
84 Hispano 20mm cannon, with 120 rounds of ammunition
85 Cannon barrel support fairing
86 Main spar
87 Mainwheel leg shock-absorber
88 Mainwheel fairing
89 Mainwheel
90 Carburettor air intake
91 Machine-gun ports
92 Gun heating pipe
93 Wingroot fillet

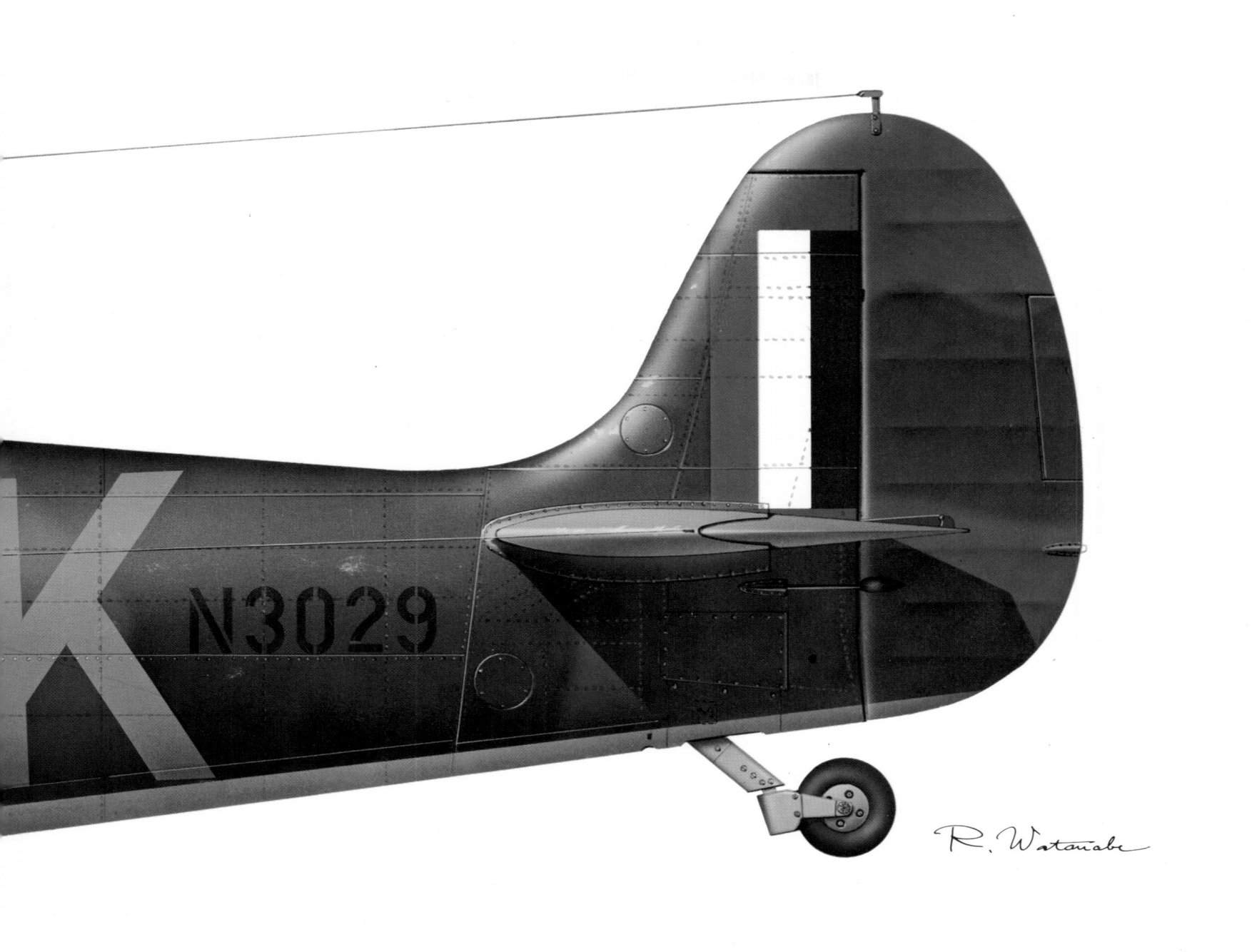

Spitfire Mk IA, N3029 'K' of 610 'County of Chester' Sqn, based at Biggin Hill. The N3029 'K' was one of the second production batch of two hundred Mk Is ordered from Supermarine in 1937. It took part in the Battle of Britain but was lost on 8 January, 1943, while being shipped overseas—after having surived four years of air combat.

1m

1 2 3 ft

lems and the inevitable lag in the introduction of some of the features of the definitive service aircraft. By September, 1939, however, the Spitfire had revealed little of its true class. Technically and operationally, the most remarkable part of the story was still to unfold.

Room for Improvement — 1

Most of the Spitfires built before mid-1942 were broadly similar, at least three major groups of modified aircraft appearing on the scene thereafter. The first group, however, can be identified by one common feature: their Merlin engines were supercharged by a single centrifugal impeller stage, and were similar enough in general layout to be interchangeable. Built in larger numbers than subsequent 'generations,' they pioneered many of the armament and systems variations later to be available on the Spitfire, and thus existed in a vast range of subtypes and variants.

The first Spitfire I variant to appear was a one-off type, and the second an improvisation, and both were capable of extremely high performance. The first was the High Speed Spitfire N17, and the second was the start of a long series of Spitfires modified for strategic reconnaissance. The different degrees of success enjoyed by the two aircraft indicate some of the Spitfire's stronger and weaker points.

The High Speed Spitfire was based on a standard aircraft, just as Germany's 463 mph He100 record-breaker was adapted from an experimental fighter, and was in sharp contrast to the purpose-built Messerschmitt Me209V1. It was the He100's run which put paid to Supermarine's hopes of the record even before any attempt was made. However, the exercise was not a complete waste of time. The airframe modification, admittedly, had little direct relevance to a production aircraft. A low-drag, curved windscreen was fitted, and the radiators were removed. A large detachable radiator bath was fitted for normal flight testing, and for the record run an enlarged coolant tank was to be used and the coolant simply allowed to boil away. The two-bladed propeller of the standard aircraft was replaced by a fine-pitch four-bladed wooden propeller optimised for high speed. The airframe was polished to achieve the smoothest possible finish, and the wingtips were clipped.

The High Speed Spitfire's engine was a harbinger of what the Merlin would later achieve under service conditions. It was a stock engine apart from strengthened connecting rods, pistons and gudgeon pins, and was not only rated at 2,160 hp for a record run but managed a 15-hour endurance test at 1,800 hp. Even with the aid of a racing cocktail similar to the brew used for the Schneider Trophy engines, this was a remarkable performance. The High Speed Spitfire was expected to attain 410 mph at sea level, slower than the maximum speed at altitude of many subsequent service Spitfires.

In November, 1939, the Photographic Development Unit (PDU, later the Photographic Reconnaissance Unit or PRU) at Heston put into service the second Spitfire I derivative, starting a series of photographic reconnaissance Spitfires. Specially converted from standard production aircraft, these were originally designated Spitfire A and B and so on. The Spitfire A was an unarmed, cleaned-up Spitfire I, but in the course of time the series was to embrace much more extensive modifications of the standard aircraft, with extra fuel and oil capacity. The PDU was led by Sidney Cotton, who had laid the foundations for aerial reconnaissance of Germany before the war in a Lockheed transport fitted with concealed cameras. The PR Spitfires benefited from this experience, and were fitted with progressively more powerful photographic equipment.

A less successful experiment was the service introduction of the Spitfire IB. Armed with four Brownings and two Mk 1 Hispano cannon of 20-mm calibre, the IB was ordered into production after trials of the new guns under the wings of a Hurricane in early 1939. (When the so-called 'B' wing carrying four guns and two cannon was introduced, the original eight-gun aircraft was retrospectively designated Spitfire IA.) Placed into service in July 1940, the Spitfire IBs soon acquired an unenviable reputation for high rates of cannon stoppages. The heavy recoil force of the opposite cannon made the aircraft virtually uncontrollable and useless as a gun platform, and the squadron chosen for the trials insisted on being re-equipped with IAs.

Production at Castle Bromwich began to build up rapidly in the second half of 1940, this facility concentrating on the Spitfire II. Powered by a Merlin XII of higher take-off power and higher rated altitude than the powerplants of Spitfire Is, the new type also featured additional armour protection for the pilot and the coolant tank. The engine was started by a cartridge-activated Coffman starter instead of an electric motor, and a constant-speed propeller was fitted as standard. Spitfire IIAs and IIBs were produced with similar armament to the IA and IB, while a few aircraft were fitted with the universal C wing which could accommodate either the A or B armament or, alternatively, four Hispano cannon. Despite the development of the Hispano to an acceptable level of reliability, however, the armament carried by most Spitfires and favoured by the squadrons was the B wing with its mix of cannon and machine guns.

If the Spitfire II was the definitive version of the first Spitfire subtype, the Spitfire V was the first version to offer a substantial increase in performance. It was also, taking the VA, VB and VC versions together, the most widely produced single Mark of the aircraft. Previous Merlin engines had been designed to accept the 85 octane fuel which was the best the RAF could guarantee during the early war years; by the end of 1940 the supply of 100 octane fuel was building up and the boost pressure from the supercharger could be increased without fear of detonation. The early Merlin had also been found to suffer from a very restricted airflow to the supercharger, and at first it was thought that modified impeller ducting necessary to solve this problem would also lengthen the engine. However, by reversing the carburettor the increase in length was cancelled out; the new Merlin 45 series was both more powerful and more efficient than its predecessors and could be installed in a similar airframe.

Most of the aircraft produced in this series were fitted with the B (four Brownings, two cannon) wing, but about 20 per cent of the output comprised eight-gun VAs and

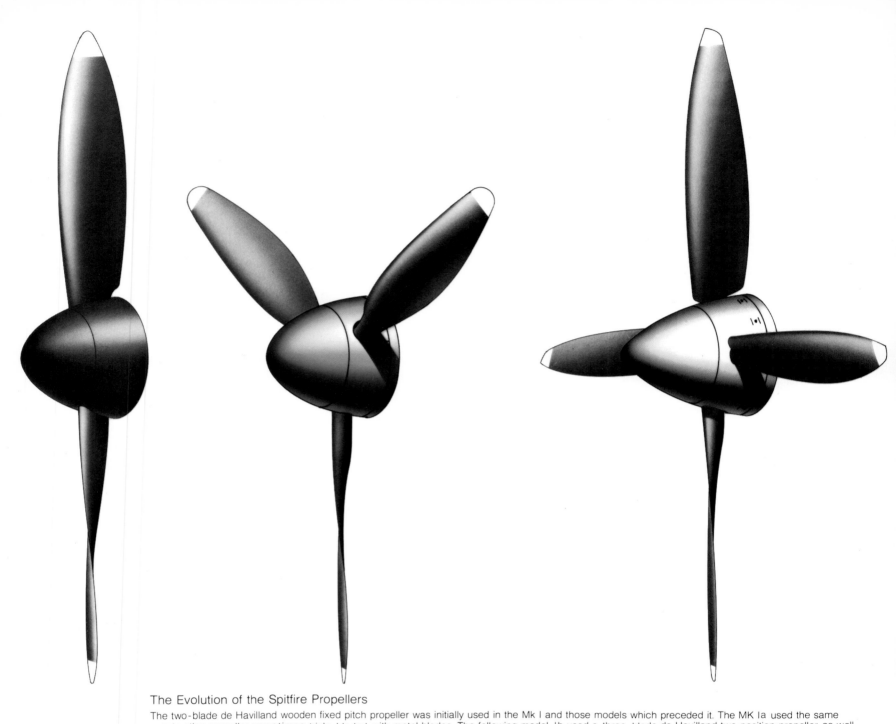

The Evolution of the Spitfire Propellers
The two-blade de Havilland wooden fixed pitch propeller was initially used in the Mk I and those models which preceded it. The MK Ia used the same construction propeller sometimes triple-bladed with metal blades. The following model, Ib used a three-blade de Havilland two-position propeller as well. The three-blade Rotol Jablo variable pitch propeller was used in the IIa. Both IIb and IIc used a three-blade de Havilland hydromatic constant speed propeller. Other aircraft using three-bladed propellers were the PR III and IV, as well as the V series.

another tenth were delivered as four-cannon VCs with additional armour and bomb pylons. A number of Spitfire Is and IIs were modified at maintenance and repair units to V standard, with some strengthening of the fuselage and installation of the Merlin 45.

The Spitfire V entered service in March, 1941, and although it was the dominant production version for most of 1941-42 at Castle Bromwich and Supermarine—by that time dispersed throughout Southern England—within two years it was outclassed as a medium-altitude fighter. Many surviving aircraft were then converted to low-level fighters, under the designation LF.V. The wingtips were removed outboard of the ailerons and a smaller supercharger impeller was fitted. The effect of the latter modification, indicated by the suffix M on the engine designation, was to allow the engine to develop more power at low level without detonation, at the same time reducing the power demands of the blower; however, the smaller impeller was incapable of maintaining full power at altitudes above 2,750 ft (838 m). Dubbed 'clipped, cropped and clapped' by their pilots, the LF.V.s were mainly used as improvised ground-attack fighters. Other Mark Vs were converted into PR.VII and PR.XIII tactical reconnaissance fighters with oblique cameras, the PR.XIII being a factory conversion.

The Spitfire V was the basis for numerous Spitfire derivatives, both successful and abortive. One of the most remarkable was the Spitfire D or PR.IV long-range reconnaissance aircraft, developed in mid-1941. Although the Spitfire had not been developed with long-range operations in mind, the legacy of the Goshawk included the torsion-box leading-edge which, with armament removed, made an impressive integral fuel tank. The addition of 133 Imp gal (605 lit) of fuel more than doubled the fuel capacity of the PR.IV and endowed it with a range of 2,000 miles (3,220 km). An enlarged oil tank was housed in a modified lower engine cowling. The long-span, low-drag wing of the Spitfire was the other contributor to this long-range performance, which

The first four-blade propeller was used on the IV. On the HF. VI the four-blade Rotol Jablo constant speed propeller was used; the four-blade Rotol hydulignum being used on PR. VIIs, F. VIIIs, F. IXs, PR. XIs and other aircraft. The first five-blade propeller was used on the XIVe. It was a Rotol constant speed model and used reinforced wooden blades. Other aircraft used five-blade propellers were the F. XVIII, the FRXVIII, the PR. XIX and the F. 21 and 22, these latter two models using a five-blade Rotol constant speed. Six-blade propellers (Rotol counter-rotating) were used on the FR.XIV, and those F.21s and F.22s equipped with the Griffon 85 engine.

combined with the high speed of the Spitfire allowed it to roam over Germany in daylight without incurring prohibitive losses.

The Spitfire V was also the basis for the Seafire, conceived in 1941 when it was realised that the carrier-based Hurricanes and Martlets of the Fleet Air Arm were no match for the latest generation of Luftwaffe fighters. The Seafire IBs were converted from existing Spitfire VBs; the IIC was a more thorough modification, built from the outset as a naval fighter but lacking folding wings. The first IICs were delivered in mid-1942. The Seafire LIIC, a low-level-optimised successor to the basic IIC with a cropped-impeller engine and a four-blade propeller (among single-stage Merlin aircraft, only Seafires had these), entered service in the following year.

The Fleet Air Arm, defending targets which at that time were invulnerable to high-altitude level bombing, attached less importance to high-altitude operations than their dry-shod brethren, and never used any Merlin derivative other than the single-stage 45 and the low-altitude 32 series. Although the Seafire had been conceived as a stopgap pending delivery in late 1943 of purpose-built American naval fighters (Grumman F6F Hellcats and Chance Vought F4U Corsairs), there was some doubt that these could be delivered on time and the development of the Seafire continued. The Seafire III was the first of the family with folding wings, a system having been devised which retained 90 per cent of the thin wing's rigidity without excessive weight increase. Most of these aircraft—built by a separate Seafire production organisation, headed by Westland—were completed as LIII low-altitude fighters with cropped-impeller engines, which served alongside the US-built fighters. The Seafire LIII was the most widely produced version of the type, and the last to enter service during the war. The Seafire LIII was also the only single-stage-engine version to feature the new exhaust stacks introduced on the later variants of the type. The replacement of collector pipes with individual ejector ports for

Merlin 60 series engine section

The Spitfire is always associated with the Merlin engine. Though it was a Rolls-Royce engine, the Griffon, which gave the plane its later boosted performance, the Merlin was its first and in some ways its most important engine. The two-stage two-speed Merlin 60 series driving four-bladed reinforced wood propellers was the initial powerplant which carried the Spitfire into the skies of Europe. Its largest drawback was its 27 litre capacity. This limited performance and led to the development of the 36.7 litre two-stage Griffon. This development had certain parallels in Germany where in an attempt to gain more power the 33.9 litre capacity of the DB 601 series was increased to 35.7 litres in the DB 605A series, and to not less than 44.5 litres in the DB 603A series.

Merlin 61	V-1650-3	V-1650-7	V-1650-9 (Merlin 100)
Take-off Power:	1380hp max 5 min	1490hp max 5 min	1830hp wet
Griffon	III, IV	65	85
Take-off Power:	1720hp	1540hp	1915hp

Rolls-Royce Merlin 61 Engine

1 Valve gear cover
2 Propeller shaft
3 Volute chamber
4 Supercharger components
5 Exit guide vane ring
6 Valve
7 Rocker arm
8 Coolant outlet connection
9 Valve spring
10 Overhead camshaft
11 Cylinder sleeve
12 Camshaft bevel-drive gear
13 Connecting rod
14 Piston and rings
15 Spark plug
16 Exhaust port
17 Tachometer drive
18 Magneto cross-shaft driving gear
19 Air intake
20 Twin choke carburettor
21 Throttle oil heating pipe
22 Crankcase lateral bolts
23 Balanced crankshaft
24 Supercharger two speed driving gear
25 Scavenge oil suction pipe
26 Oil pump
27 Reduction gear
28 Propeller constant speed unit
29 Automatic boost control unit

each cylinder was credited with a 4 mph (6.5 km/hr) increase in maximum speed.

Another derivative of the Mark V was the first pressurised Spitfire, developed to counter expected high-altitude bombing. The Spitfire VI was fitted with a Marshall cabin blower and a sealed, non-jettisonable canopy, together with extended, more pointed wingtips. Rated altitude of its Merlin 47 engine, however, was only 14,000 ft (4,270 m), limiting the performance of the Spitfire VI to the point where it was regarded as a stopgap pending development of the more extensively modified Mk VII, and only 100 Spitfire VIs were built.

The long family of Spitfire V descendants included some smaller subgroups; among these were the PR.VI or Spitfire F and the PV.VII Spitfire G, field modifications of the basic type. There was also the small batch of Spitfire V floatplanes, converted in 1942. The Spitfire had been earmarked for float conversion in early 1940, in a panic programme to provide a fighter which could fly from fjords in defence of Norway. One conversion, known as the 'Narvik Nightmare,' was completed but never flown: a Spitfire I fitted with floats developed for the lumbering Blackburn Roc turret fighter, its performance would have been poor. The Spitfire V conversion, by contrast, was designed by the Supermarine team and produced what was probably the best float fighter of the war, even compared with the purpose-built Japanese Kawanishi N1K1 'Kyofu.' Specially designed floats were attached to the wings by slender cantilever pylons with no cross-bracing, and the water and air handling of the conversion was reported to be excellent. The 11 ft 3 in (3.43 m) four-blade propeller was the largest fitted to any Spitfire.

The three Mk V conversions completed were ferried

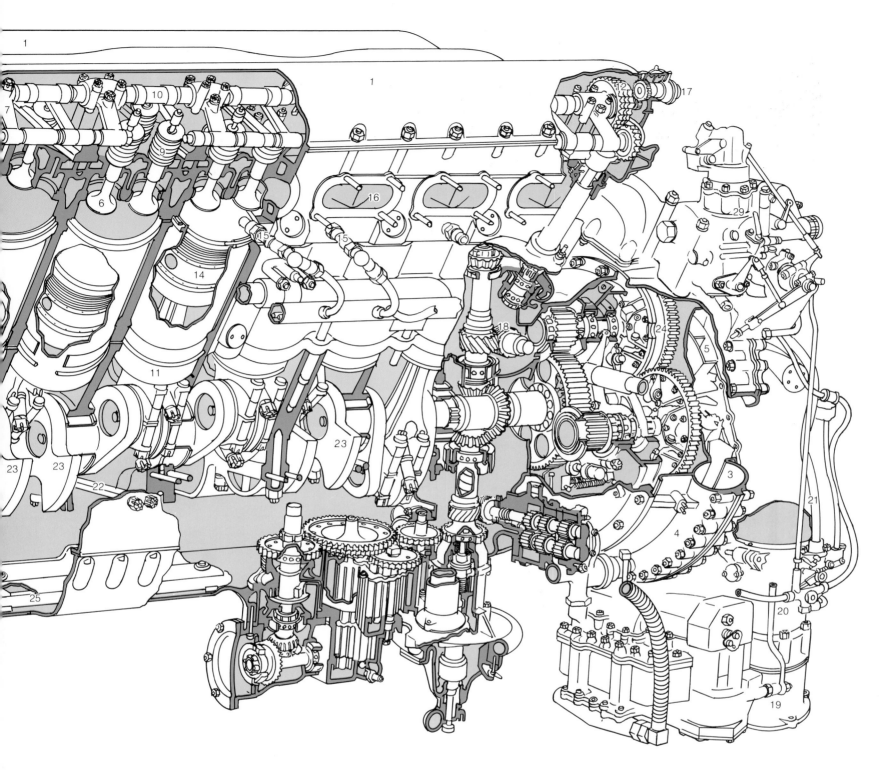

in great secrecy to Alexandria in the autumn of 1943. In an exercise worthy of the grandest fictional feats of arms, it was intended to operate the Spitfires from an uninhabited Greek island to harry Luftwaffe transport aircraft, supplying and controlling them by submarine. However, the German counter-attack in the Aegean overran the intended launching point for the operation while the floatplanes were still working up on the Great Bitter Lake, and the plan was abandoned.

One of the last derivatives of the Spitfire V to appear was one of the most unusual and was certainly not intended as a production version. It is not quite clear when or how Spitfire V EN380 fell intact into German hands, but in November, 1943, it was modified by the experimental and flight-test department of Daimler-Benz to accept a DB605A-1 engine and VDM propeller in a modified Bf 109G cowling, together with German instruments and a 24v electrical sys-

tem. The aircraft as modified was reported to be far more pleasant to fly than the Bf 109, particularly in take-off and landing. It was slower than the Bf 109 at low and medium altitudes but could climb much faster, despite the fact that the engine was some 200 lb (90 kg) heavier than the original Merlin. The DB605 Spitfire was destroyed during a USAAF bombing raid in August, 1944.

The development of the Spitfire V had left the Spitfire more heavily armed and better protected than the aircraft envisaged in 1935. Its performance, however, had not greatly improved; the higher speeds at low level attained by modified LF.Vs were in the future when that type entered service. By that time, moreover, development along a number of parallel lines was under way, with a view to further exploiting the immense potential, by now being appreciated, of the basic design.

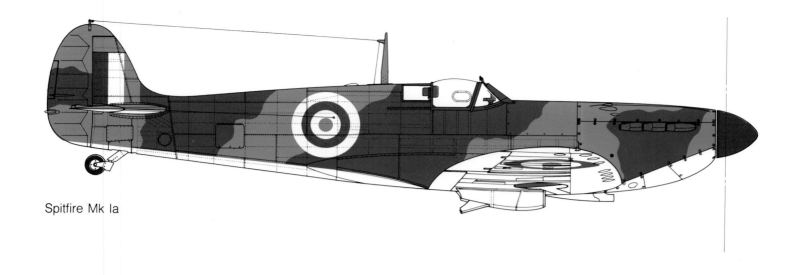

Spitfire Mk Ia

Room for improvement — 2: Which stage next?

Aircraft development in wartime seldom follows a logical sequence, and the Spitfire typifies this tendency more than any other type does. Repeatedly, developments were started only to be overhauled by improvisations stimulated by urgent operational needs, the improvisation being sufficiently successful to postpone the production of the original development still further. To comprehend the life cycle of the aircraft, it is necessary to look at the options available for short-term and medium-term developments in 1939 and 1940, which could be considered for application to future production aircraft once the crisis of the Battle was over.

One early proposal was to produce a generally cleaned-up version of the original design. Relatively simple modifications such as switching from a fixed to a retractable tailwheel, and the addition of small doors to cover the retracted mainwheels (semi-exposed on the Spitfire I) would yield a useful increase in maximum speed for a small increase in cost and complexity. Also becoming available at that time was the Merlin XX series engine, using the same supercharger as the 45 series with a two-speed mechanical drive. This engine could work to its full potential over a wider range of altitudes than the single-speed engine of the original Spitfire, and could be installed with only minor modifications.

The Merlin XX and other refinements mentioned above were fitted to the Spitfire III, which appeared in the form of a single prototype late in 1939. However, that was not the most auspicious moment to present the Ministries with a new version of the Spitfire; logical as the development of the Spitfire III might be, deliveries of the standard aircraft were still behind schedule and the introduction of more modifications could only delay production. Plans to build the III at Castle Bromwich were cancelled, and it was the Mark II version of the better established Hurricane that received the first Merlin XX powerplants. When an improved Spitfire was ordered, it was the Spitfire V, with an almost unmodified airframe and an engine which achieved similar results to the XX with less modification and weight. By the time that production constraints permitted consideration of more radi-

cal derivatives of the Spitfire, other developments had improved vastly on the single-stage, two-speed Merlin XX.

The first radical change to be embarked upon was the second to be used. In 1939, Rolls-Royce and Supermarine had collaborated closely in the design of an engine which, although much larger in capacity than the Merlin, would fit with few airframe modifications in aircraft designed for the smaller engine. This placed very tight restrictions on length (because an engine as long for its capacity as the Merlin would have made a re-engined fighter nose-heavy) and frontal area, and after considerable work on the mock-up the design of the Griffon was frozen. The Griffon had been conceived as a high-power, low-altitude engine, and a heavily armed low-level intercepter version of the Spitfire was designed around it. This prototype was tested with a wing carrying a mock-up of a six-Hispano armament. It was originally designated Spitfire IV, but the designation PR.IV had been allotted before the first Griffon-powered aircraft flew. Incorporating the design refinements of the Spitfire III, this aircraft became the sole Spitfire XX.

The Mark XX never went into production. Instead it became the first of the ultimate Mark 20 series Spitfires, another line of development which was to be largely overhauled by improvisation. Designed to overcome the Spitfire's only major weakness, these aircraft underwent a protracted gestation and finally entered service as the war drew to a close. In concept, however, they antedated most of the wartime production aircraft.

Early trials at Martlesham Heath with the Spitfire I had revealed that the ailerons became increasingly heavy at high diving speeds, and a modified design of fabric aileron was introduced during Spitfire I production to alleviate the problem. However, the unexpected development of the 'diving race' style of air combat in wartime took the Spitfire into the high-speed regime where its lateral control became increasingly heavy. The Spitfire V introduced metal ailerons of the Frise type, in which the leading edge was shaped to aid the upward deflection of the aileron, but this was still no more than a palliative. The 'clipped' wings of LF Spitfires were intended to reduce rolling inertia, but also worsened performance at altitude.

Investigation of the problem revealed by late 1940

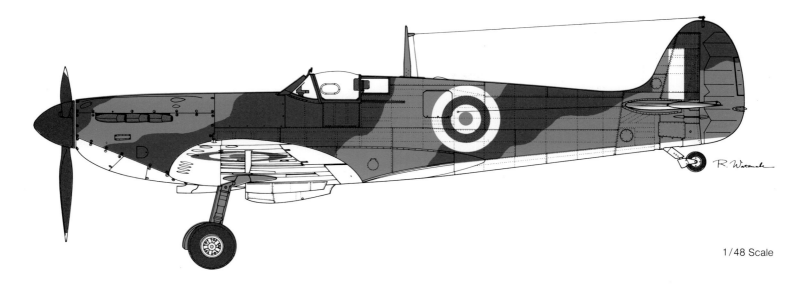

that the existing Spitfire wing, with its simple torsion-box leading-edge, could not be fitted with more powerful ailerons without encountering 'reversal,' a phenomenon in which the aileron twists the wing as a tab deflects an aileron, reversing the control input. The design of a new wing with plain ailerons and a structure of multiple torsion boxes was started, and this was to be combined with the Griffon engine of the Spitfire XX to produce the Spitfire XXI (generally written as 21). A parallel if slightly later development was an alternative new wing based on the 'laminar-flow' symmetrical aerofoil already in use on the North American P-51 Mustang, deeper in section than the Spitfire wing but offering similar performance. Neither wing retained the original elliptical platform of the earlier Spitfires, but Mitchell's classically beautiful shape had more life in it than many people imagined.

The development that was to have most influence on the wartime Spitfire, unexpectedly extending the production life of the basic airframe, originated during 1940, when the Air Staff became increasingly interested in the threats and opportunities presented by the possibility of aircraft operations above 40,000 feet (12,190 m). It has to be recognized that the Air Ministry went a little overboard in its enthusiasm for high-altitude aircraft. High-altitude, pressurized versions of the Wellington bomber were built, as well as two specialised high-altitude interceptors; one of the latter, the Westland Welkin, was put into production but never fired a shot in anger. However, the high-altitude requirement produced one very useful result in the shape of the special Merlin engine developed for the Wellington and Welkin.

This, the Merlin 60, differed from its predecessors in possessing a two-stage supercharger to achieve much higher boost levels and maintain power at high altitudes. With a two-speed drive, it could also produce high power at lower levels. In addition, the Merlin 60 featured an 'aftercooler': an air cooler between the supercharger and the inlet manifold which lowered the temperature of the air and increased the boost pressure which could be achieved without detonation. The Merlin 60 had vastly better high-altitude performance than the earlier Merlins, and was significantly better at all but the lowest altitudes. However, in the long run its most significant attribute was the ease with which it could be applied to the standard aircraft.

Room for improvement—3: A Successful Panic

Understandably, in view of the apparently increasing danger that the Luftwaffe would make a large-scale switch to high-altitude bombing from outside the reach of conventional fighters, the first version of the Spitfire to be ordered into production with the two-stage-supercharged Merlin was a high-altitude type. Predictably, in view of the tortuous path taken by the development of the type, the first actually to enter service was the third to be allotted a Mark number; it was an improvisation, and it was to be built in greater numbers than any other version of the type except the Spitfire V series.

In 1941, Spitfire pilots returned from fighter sweeps over Northern France reporting encounters with a new and formidable German radial-engined fighter. This, the Focke-Wulf Fw 190, was superior by a substantial margin to the Spitfire V, only then entering service, and with the increasing employment of the new German fighter the development of a version of the Spitfire offering superior straight-line and climbing performance at all altitudes became a matter of urgency.

Development of two parallel Spitfire versions combining the airframe refinements pioneered on the prototype Spitfire III with the Merlin 60 engine was under way, but it was considered more important to speed up as far as possible the shift of Spitfire production from the Mk V to a more potent aircraft. In theory, the greater power and speed of a Spitfire with the new engine would demand a certain amount of strengthening to the airframe, while the four-blade airscrew needed to absorb the greater output of the new engine would call for a slightly larger tailfin to counteract its destabilising effect. None of these modifications was applied to the Spitfire IX, which in its standard production form was virtually identical to the Spitfire V aft of the firewall, apart from the aftercooler in the enlarged port radiator duct. Ahead of it, all was changed, with a 1,710 hp Merlin 60, a four-blade Rotol airscrew and the more efficient multiple ejector exhausts. The reduction in structural load safety factors inherent in such a simple modification was accepted as the price of a speed gain which included an improvement in level speed of 70 mph (112 km/hr), or upwards of 20 per cent, at all altitudes. Climb, acceleration and sustained turning ability were increased in proportion: in modern terms, the Spitfire IX enjoyed higher 'specific excess power' than the Mark V.

Most of the 5,600 Spitfire IXs were built as LF.IXs, their supercharger gearing optimised for best performance below 6,000 feet (1,830 m); less than a quarter had the medium-altitude-rated Merlin, and a tenth of the IXs built were HF models with engines rated at 22,500 ft (6,850 m) in top gear. (None had 'cropped' superchargers, so all were multi-level fighters unlike the LF.V.) Although none of the Spitfire IXs was actually delivered with clipped wingtips, the variant followed the Spitfire V in being so modified in the field or at maintenance units once more advanced versions had taken over the task of medium-altitude interception. Some later aircraft were also fitted with a larger tailfin. The wing of the Spitfire IX was basically that of the VC, production of the A and B wings having ceased. The C wings of the Mark IX invariably carried the two-cannon, four-Browning armament; in 1944, however, the E wing was introduced and replaced the four 0.303 fin (7.7 mm) guns with a pair of 0.5 in (12.7 mm) weapons, and this equipped later Spitfire IXs. An advantage of the E wing was that the guns were housed in two bays instead of six, simplifying maintenance.

The Spitfire IX was the progenitor of the usual quota of experiments, two of the most remarkable being concerned with marine operations. In the United Kingdom, one of the conversion kits developed for the Spitfire V float-plane was applied to a single Spitfire IX. The Spitfire IX floatplane appeared some time after the plans to operate the marine Mark V from hidden bases in the Mediterranean had been abandoned, and it is not clear for what theatre the aircraft was intended; however, it was unquestionably the fastest float fighter ever built, with a maximum speed of 377 mph (607 km/hr), and helped to inspire development of the Saunders-Roe SR.A1 flying-boat fighter ordered in 1944.

Another maritime experiment involved one of the 1,288 Spitfire IXs delivered to the Soviet Union, which in 1947 was converted for tests of a rail-type catapult similar to that used for British Hurricane-equipped CAM (Catapult-Armed Merchantman) ships in the Battle of the Atlantic. This Soviet venture into maritime air power was apparently a failure, and was not proceeded with.

Rarely can any aircraft have absorbed a 70 per cent power increase with as little external and internal modification as the Spitfire did between the Mark I and the Mark IX, and certainly no aircraft has exploited it so well. The advantage in power which the Mark IX enjoyed over the V is well illustrated by the floatplane version; with two massive pontoons slung below the wings, the Mark IX was still slightly faster than the landplane Mark V. The implications in terms

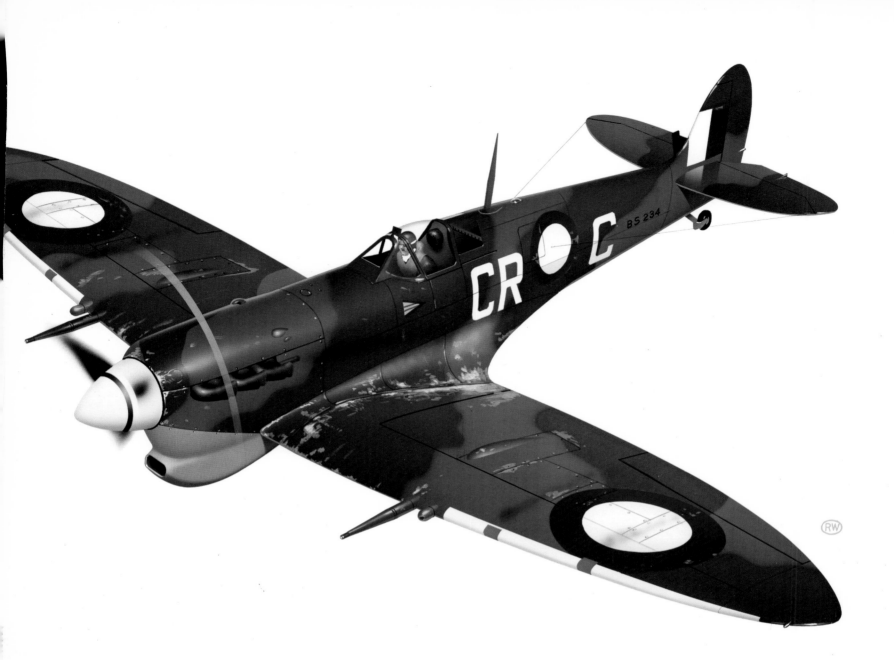

▲ Spitfire Mk VC

Flown by Wing Commander Clive R. Caldwell, probably the
most celebrated of all Australian fighter pilots, Wing Leader No. 1
Fighter Wing, Royal Australian Air Force; Darwin, Australia,
1942–43. Serial BS234.

Rolls-Royce Merlin 45/46/50/50A engines: 1,470 hp

Performance:

Max speed:	374 mph at 13,000 ft (602 km/h at 3960 m)
Time to 20,000 ft (6100 m): 7 min 30 sec	
Service ceiling:	37,000 ft (11,300 m)
Range:	470 mls (760 km)
	1,135 mls (1830 km) with 175 Imp. gal (796 ltr)
Weight:	6,785 lb (3078 kg)

Dimensions:

Span:	36 ft 10 in (11.323 m)
Length:	29 ft 11 in (9.116 m)
Height:	11 ft 5½ in (3.491 m)
	Airscrew vertical, 11 ft 4¾ in (3.472 m)
Wing area:	242 sq.ft (22.3 m²)

Armament:	2(4) x 20 mm Hispano-Suiza cannon
	4 x .303 Browning machine-guns

20 mm Hispano-Suiza Cannon

The original design known as 20 mm Hispano-Suiza Birkigt Type 404. British interest expressed 1936, negotiations to purchase six guns concluded same year, deliveries effected early 1937. After positive tests in the same year the British accepted a HS proposal to build a special plant in Britain to manufacture a minumum of 400 guns. Guns manufactured in Britain were initially known simply as 20-mm Hispano-Suiza Type 404; later, 20-mm Automatic Gun Mk I (etc.).

Mk I: Initial British production from French drawings. Small series only due to difficulties with (metric) drawings.

Mk II: British manufacture from new (British) drawings which included various minor changes and improvements to suit British manufacturing methods and large-scale production.

Mk III: Designed to have fabricated gun body for cheaper production and reduced weight. Test examples only: no production.

Mk IV: Identical to Mk II but barrel 12 in shorter; also, a shoulder 9 in further to rear. Intended mainly as turret gun, but only small number produced.

Mk V: British development of original French design.
Incorporated various minor improvements. 25%
lighter than Mk II, 50% higher rate of fire, barrel 12 in
shorter. In service as fixed and turret installation
weapon.

▼ Spitfire L.F. Mk VB

Flown by Wing Commander I.R. 'Widge' Gleed, No. 601
Sqn, AR502. A Battle of Britain veteran, Gleed had at least
15 victories to his credit when he failed to return from a 16
April, 1943, fighter sweep.

Rolls-Royce Merlin 45M/50M/55M engines: 1,585 hp

Performance:

Max speed:	369 mph at 19,500 ft (594 km/h at 5950 m)
Time to 5000 ft (1520 m): 1 min 36 sec	
Service ceiling:	36,500 ft (11,100 m)
Range:	470 mls (760 km) with 85 Imp.gal (386 ltr)
Weight:	6,650 lb (3016 kg)

Dimensions:

Span:	32 ft 7 in (9.928 m)
Length:	29 ft 11 in (9.116 m)
Height:	11 ft 5½ in (3.491 m)
	Airscrew vertical, 11 ft 4¾ in (3.472 m)
Wing area:	231 sq.ft (21.3 m²)
Armament:	2 x 20 mm Hispano-Suiza cannon
	4 x .303 Browning machine-guns

▼ Spitfire H.F. Mk VI

No. 616 'South Yorkshire' Squadron, June, 1942. BS111.

Rolls-Royce Merlin 47/49 engines: 1,415 hp

Performance:

Max speed:	364 mph at 22,000 ft (586 km/h at 6700 m)
Time to 20,000 ft (6100 m): 8 min	
Service ceiling:	40,000 ft (12,200 m)
Range:	510 mls (820 km)
Weight:	6,797 lb (3083 kg)

Dimensions:

Span:	40 ft 2 in (12.239 m)
Length:	29 ft 11 in (9.116 m)
Height:	11 ft 5½ in (3.491 m)
	Airscrew vertical, 11 ft 4¾ in (3.472 m)
Wing area:	248.5 sq.ft (22.9 m²)

Armament: 2 x 20 mm Hispano-Suiza cannon
4 x .303 Browning machine-guns

20mm (British) Hispano Mk I

Length of gun:	93.7 in (2380 mm)
Weight (less feeder):	102 lb (46.27 kg)
Rate of fire:	600–650 rpm
Muzzle velocity:	2850 ft/sec (868.7 m/sec)
Ammo feed:	Drum; later Chatellerault automatic spring-wound feeder
Length of barrel:	67.5 in (1714.5 mm)
Weight of barrel:	47.5 lb (21.55 kg)
Bore:	8 grooves, RH twist
Rifling length:	63.08 in (1602 mm)
Cartridge:	20 mm Hispano-Suiza (M75 series)

20 mm (British) Hispano Mk V

Length of gun:	77 in (1955.8 mm)
Weight of gun:	99.5 lb (45.1 kg)
Rate of fire:	700–750 rpm
Muzzle velocity:	2850 ft/sec (868.7 m/sec)
Ammo feed:	Automatic spring-wound feeder using metallic links
Length of barrel:	52.5 in (1333.5 mm)
Weight of barrel:	26 1/4 lb (12.1 kg)
Bore:	9 grooves, RH twist
Cartridge:	20 mm Hispano-Suiza (M75 series)

Browing .303 Machine Gun Mk II

Calibre:	.303 in (7.7 mm)
Belt feed:	Recoil operated
Weight of gun:	21.9 lb (9.93 kg)
Rate of fire:	1200 rpm (cyclic)
Weight of bullet:	.022 lb (10.0 g)
Muzzle velocity:	2600 ft/sec (811 m/sec)

▲ Spitfire Mk 24

Similar to the Mark 22 (from which several had been converted)
the Spitfire 24 had internal differences, among them the ability
to carry eight 60 lb rockets. No. 80 Squadron was the sole Royal
Air Force unit to use this version. It flew Mark 24s until
January, 1952, and was the last fighter unit to operate Spitfires.

Rolls-Royce Griffon 61/85 engines: 2,050 hp

Performance:

Max speed:	454 mph at 26,000 ft (731 km/h at 7900 m)
Time to 20,000 ft (6100 m): 8 min	
Service ceiling:	43,500 ft (13,250 m)
Range:	490 mls with 120 Imp. gal (790 km with 546 ltr)
	640 mls with 150 Imp. gal (1030 km with 682 ltr)
	880 mls with 210 Imp. gal (1420 km with 955 ltr)
Weight:	9,900 lb (4490 kg)

Dimensions:

Span:	36 ft 11 in (11.249 m)
Length:	32 ft 11 in (9.801 m)
Height:	Airscrew vertical, 13 ft 6 in (4.114 m)
Wing area:	244 sq.ft (22.5 m²)
Armament:	4 x 20 mm Hispano-Suiza cannon

of the ability of the Mark IX to climb and accelerate in combat are clear: and this was an improvisation?

Once the Spitfire IX was established at the massive but inflexible plant at Castle Bromwich, the smaller but more versatile Supermarine production group could turn its attention back to the original two-stage-engine derivatives which had been overhauled with such good effect by the Mark IX. The first to appear was the high-altitude Spitfire VII (a different aircraft altogether from the confusingly designated PR.VII, which was a field-modified Spitfire VA), combining the long-span wing and pressure cabin of the interim Mark VI high-altitude fighter with the two-stage engine and other design refinements such as a sliding hood (the pilot of the earlier Mark VI could not escape in an emergency), a retractable tailwheel and a stronger airframe.

After 140 Mark VIIs had been built, it was decided that the high-altitude threat had receded and the pressurized aircraft was replaced in production by the unpressurized Mark VIII, which essentially amounted to a refined and strengthened Spitfire IX with a slightly higher speed due to its retractable tailwheel. It also differed from the Mark IX in being delivered with extended-span and clipped wings as well as the standard planform. Most of the Mark VIIIs had clipped wings and low-level Merlins and at least some of the type had four 20-mm Hispano cannon. Later aircraft shared the taller, more pointed tailfin of later Spitfire IXs. Supermarine delivered 1,650 examples of the Mark VIII before it was superseded by Griffon-powered versions.

Logical offshoots of the two-stage-engined Spitfires were the high-altitude, long-range PR.X and PR.XI reconnaissance aircraft, combining the extra fuel tankage developed for the Spitfire D/PR.IV with the two-stage Merlin and the refined airframe of the Mark VIII. As readers of this history will now have come to expect, the Mark XI preceded the Mark X into service. In fact only 16 of the pressurized Mark X Spitfires were delivered, most PR sorties being flown in unpressurized Mark XIs (of which 471 were delivered) despite the extremely high altitudes of which the lightened, highly polished aircraft were capable. Production of the Mark XI started in 1942 and the Mark Xs followed in 1944.

By 1944 the Griffon-powered Spitfires were in production, within the Supermarine organisation, but Castle Bromwich was being held ready to produce the new-generation Spitfire 21 and development of this aircraft was taking longer than expected. This doubtless was part of the inspiration for the Spitfire XVI, a low-level fighter-bomber powered by a Packard-built Merlin 266—in fact, the only difference between a late-production Spitfire LF.IX and an early Mark XVI was the production source of its engine. Both were designated Type 361 by Supermarine. Most of the XVIs featured clipped E-type wings, and a substantial proportion of them featured the all-round-vision canopy and cut-down rear deck tested on a Mark VIII. This allowed the deletion of the rear-view mirror and slightly reduced the drag of the aircraft. The later XVIs also featured the taller fin of later Merlin-powered Spitfires and a low-drag whip aerial replacing the mast type of earlier aircraft. Castle Bromwich built 1,054 Spitfire XVIs, making the Type 361 Spitfire IX/XVI the most widely built *type* of Spitfire, although the Mark V was the most abundant Mark. By the time the XVI gave way to the Mark 21 the war was almost over.

The termination of Spitfire XVI production brought

Following the successful trials with three Spitfire Mk V floatplane conversions, Folland built the Type 385 Spitfire IX floatplane conversion in 1943. Only one example was completed and test-flown.

(Imperial War Museum)

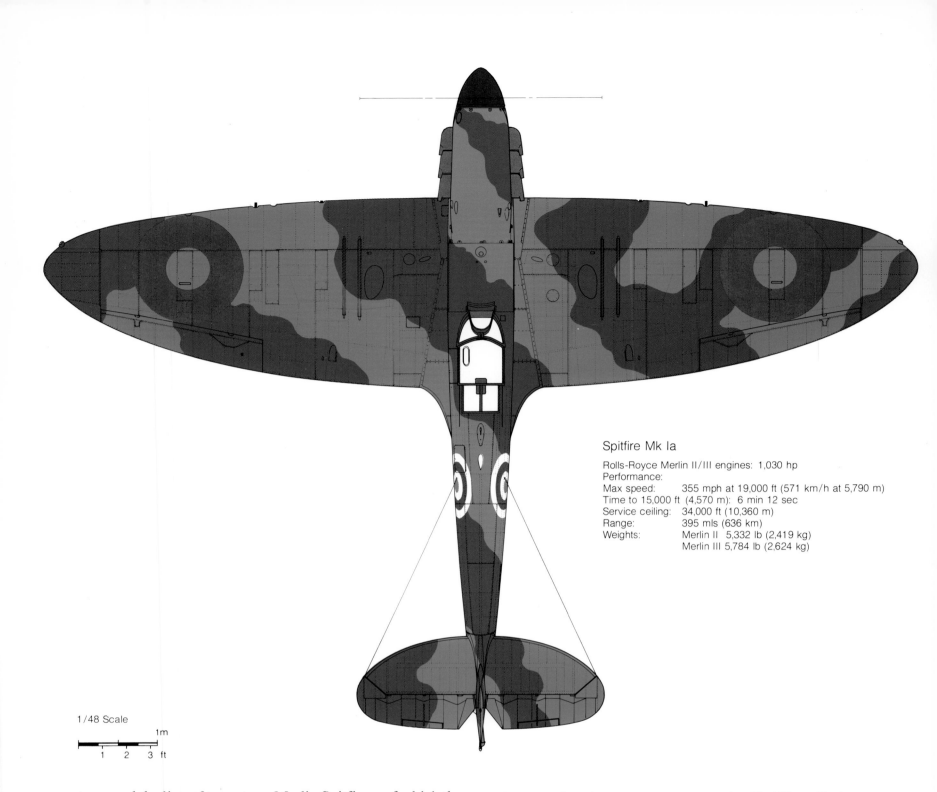

Spitfire Mk Ia

Rolls-Royce Merlin II/III engines: 1,030 hp
Performance:
Max speed: 355 mph at 19,000 ft (571 km/h at 5,790 m)
Time to 15,000 ft (4,570 m): 6 min 12 sec
Service ceiling: 34,000 ft (10,360 m)
Range: 395 mls (636 km)
Weights: Merlin II 5,332 lb (2,419 kg)
  Merlin III 5,784 lb (2,624 kg)

1/48 Scale

1m

1   2   3 ft

to an end the line of two-stage-Merlin Spitfires, of which the vast majority had been IXs and XVIs stemming directly from the original conception of a minimally modified Spitfire V. These versions, identified by their fixed tailwheels, outnumbered the 'definitive' Mark VII and its variants by three to one, ample evidence were it needed of the enormous capacity of Castle Bromwich. On the debit side, the XVI appears to have been a stopgap, put into production when the Merlin-powered Spitfire was falling increasingly far behind fighters of later conception and used mainly for ground attack. However, the development of the Spitfire IX was astonishing proof of the potential for development designed into the first prototype Spitfire I, aerodynamically almost identical. And even if the Merlin had reached the peak of what it could achieve on 100/130 octane petrol, the Spitfire—by now primarily identified as a short-range air-to-air fighter, or 'air-superiority fighter' in modern terms—still had some way to go.

Room for improvement—4: Griffon Spit

The big Griffon engine, 36 per cent larger in capacity than the Merlin and inherently more powerful by half than its smaller ancestor, had nonetheless been conceived as a powerplant suitable for the Spitfire from its earliest days. The installation of the engine in a Spitfire airframe was basically simple, but the modification of the airframe to take full advantage of the extra power was another matter. The development was also to some extent outpaced by the continuing increases in the power of the Merlin obtained through design refinements and improved supercharging. Such technology could, of course, be applied directly to the very similar Griffon, but the potential output of the larger engine at such ratings demanded innovation in both airframe and propeller design. There was thus a tendency for the development of Griffon-Spitfires to be viewed as a long-term activity while Merlin improvements

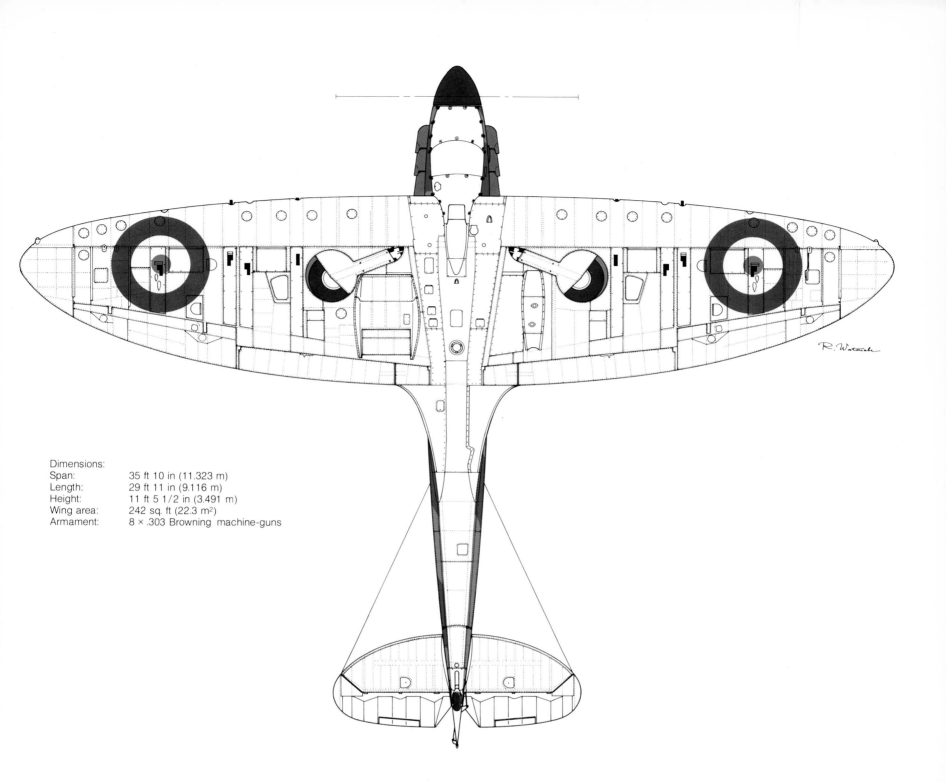

Dimensions:
Span: 35 ft 10 in (11.323 m)
Length: 29 ft 11 in (9.116 m)
Height: 11 ft 5 1/2 in (3.491 m)
Wing area: 242 sq. ft (22.3 m²)
Armament: 8 × .303 Browning machine-guns

filled the gap until the ultimate Griffon variant should become available.

Given these attitudes, it was logical that the Spitfire IV or XX should be regarded as a technology demonstrator for the improved Supermarine Type 356 or Spitfire 21. However, in the summer of 1942 the Luftwaffe adopted a new tactic: high-speed, low-level nuisance raids on targets in Southern England by aircraft such as the Fw 190A and Me210. The new Spitfire IX lacked the speed to intercept these raiders successfully at low level, its highly supercharged engine being most effective at higher altitudes. However, it pointed the way to the first Griffon-powered production Spitfire, which entered service in early 1943 with two home-defence squadrons in Southern England. This, the Spitfire XII, was strictly an improvisation, and represented one of the more marked bars sinister in the fighter's lineage: Of the 100 Mark XIIs built by Supermarine, half used Spitfire VC airframes and the rest were based on Spitfire VIIIs, all of which were converted before assembly. Clipped wingtips were standard. Externally distinguished by asymmetric underwing radiators similar to those of the Spitfire V, the XII was the only land-based Spitfire variant to feature the single-stage-supercharged Griffon; the absence of an aftercooler between the supercharger and the engine accounted for the small port radiator. Another peculiarity of the Griffon was that the propeller turned in the opposite direction to that of the Merlin, creating some traps for the newly converted Merlin pilot.

Although a two-stage Griffon was expected to be the powerplant for the definitive Griffon-Spitfire, the single-stage, two-speed engine developed for the Mark XII was suited to the Fleet Air Arm's requirement for a low/medium-altitude interceptor. The Seafire XV was more akin to a navalised Spitfire XII than any other variant, with folding wings similar to those of the Seafire III. In the course of Seafire XV production the change was made from the A-frame arrester hook, which was attached beneath the aft fuselage and tended to tip the aircraft forward on arrest, to a 'sting' hook at the extreme tail. The sting necessitated a new rudder with a higher base and broader chord. Additionally, the last batch of Seafire XVs built by Westland featured the cut-down rear fuselage and all-round-vision bubble hood introduced on all Spitfire production lines in 1944-45. The Griffon-Seafire missed the war, reaching operational squadrons in September, 1945.

Meanwhile, the introduction into service of the two-stage Griffon had taken an unexpected turn. Six Spitfire VIIIs had been allocated to test and develop this engine for the Spitfire 21, one of these aircraft being the first Spitfire to feature a contra-rotating propeller, and trials of these aircraft proved so successful that it was decided to produce yet another interim variant in the Supermarine organization, to yield a faster medium-altitude Spitfire for the RAF until Castle Bromwich commenced Spitfire 21 deliveries. Perhaps predictably, this type was to be produced in greater numbers than any other Griffon-Spitfire.

The Mark VIII adaptation was known as the Spitfire XIV, entering service in the first days of 1944. The two-stage Griffon 65 drove a five-blade airscrew, and the airframe was similar to that of the Mark VIII with the exception of some strengthening and the enlargement of the fin and rudder to counteract the higher solidity of the propeller. The Supermarine-built Mark XIV was roughly contemporary with the Castle Bromwich-built, Merlin-powered Mark XVI and underwent similar changes during its production life, the most important being the introduction of the E-type wing, bubble hood and whip aerial. Nearly half the Mark XIVs were completed as FR.XIV reconnaissance-fighters with clipped wingtips and oblique F.24 camera installations in the rear fuselage in addition to full fighter armament, this dual-purpose configuration becoming increasingly popular with the British services.

There was still a need for unarmed, specialised long-range photo-reconnaissance aircraft, and the Spitfire's capability in this role attained its ultimate expression in the PR.XIX, the only Griffon-powered strategic reconnaissance version of the type. Like most of the PR variants, the Mark XIX was a hybrid, combining the fuselage of the Spitfire XIV with the high-fuel-capacity wing evolved from that of the Spitfire V and used on the PR.X and PR.XI. A few unpressurised pre-production aircraft were followed by 225 pressurised production aircraft, which appeared in time to operate in both main war theatres. Due to pressurised cabins and the fact that stern attack from above was considered unlikely (the Spitfire XIX penetrated defences at altitudes of 49,000 ft (15,000 m) during post-war exercises) the PR.XIX retained the raised rear decking and Malcolm hood throughout its production life, and possessed the distinction of being the last Spitfire to see front-line operational service.

A less successful development was the Spitfire XVIII, a high-weight version in which the original 'telescopic' mainspar was replaced by a single extrusion and the undercarriage was strengthened and increased in track. The fuel capacity of the type, which had been steadily increased by the addition of small extra tanks in successive versions as the power and fuel consumption of the powerplant was stepped up, was further augmented by extra rear-fuselage and wing tanks. Production delays due to the new wing spar caused the XVIII to miss the war, the first examples of the type being delivered in mid-1945—deliveries running behind those of the more advanced Spitfire 21. Like the XIV, the XVIII (often, after 1945, written Mark 18) was delivered in fighter and fighter-reconnaissance versions, 200 of the 300 aircraft delivered being FR.XVIIIs. Most of the type were delivered into storage, some entering service in the late 1940s.

The Mark XVIII/18 had a maritime counterpart in the Seafire XVII/17, similarly representing a beefed-up, higher-fuel-capacity development of its predecessor and, like the Mark XVIII/18, entering service after the war. One of the advantages of the stiffer landing gear of the Seafire 17 (which retained the single-stage engine and four-blade propeller of the XV) was increased deck clearance, particularly at high weights; the increased weight and larger propeller of the Griffon had conspired to produce a great many chipped decks and bent blades, and the stiffer undercarriage conferred a great improvement in deck handling. The Seafire 17 super-

PR Mk XIX 2305hp Griffon-powered unarmed photo-reconnaissance variant. After operating over Europe during the last weeks of the war, the PR XIX appeared in the Far East.

(Imperial War Museum)

seded the XV as the sole front-line fighter in FAA service in 1947, US-built carrier fighters having retired by that time.

Once again, with the development of the Spitfire XIV, the Supermarine fighter had shown that the basic wing shape and structure could be taken further than the theoretical stiffness limits might suggest, there being little to choose in terms of performance between the Mark XIV and the more advanced, much more radically modified Mark 21. In fact, the Mark XIV was close to the ultimate in pure flying performance, although increasing speed and weight was beginning to take its toll of the type's handling qualities. Considering that the Spitfire was now absorbing the power of two Merlin Is, however, this degradation in handling quality might be regarded as understandable; and at least the Spitfire XIV was available as a defence against Fi103 flying bombs and new jet fighters while the teething troubles of the Mark 21 were still being eradicated.

Room for improvement—5: The New Look

According to the design numbers applied by Supermarine, the Spitfire Mark 21 was the first major version of the type on the drawing boards after the Mark V, preceding the Mark IX and following closely on the limited-production high-altitude Mark VII. Given this background, it is perhaps hardly surprising that in its early days there was some question as to whether such a radically redesigned aircraft should be a Spitfire at all, and other names—including Victor—were considered. By the time the Spitfire 21 appeared, the basic aircraft had advanced so far that grounds for renaming the type no longer existed.

The design of a completely new wing for the Spitfire, similar in general characteristics to that of the existing aircraft but with a completely new structure to withstand the torsional loads imposed by more sensitive ailerons, was under way in earnest by early 1942. Whereas the ailerons of previous Spitfires had been balanced by area ahead of the hinge line, those of the new Type 356 were plain and devoid of aerodynamic balance. Instead the pilot's controls were

connected to tabs on the trailing edge of each aileron, so that the surface itself was actuated aerodynamically. The wing structure was changed to incorporate multiple torsion boxes, but in the process the classic elliptical wing was modified to a more angular planform which could accommodate the more complex structure without too many production difficulties. The more effective ailerons were expected to eliminate the need for clipped wingtips and to improve high-altitude performance it was intended that the Type 356 should be fitted as standard with the extended wingtips of the Marks VI, VII and HF. VIII.

Evolving in parallel with the new elliptical wing, but with a slightly later schedule, was a more radically revised wing using a 'laminar-flow' section in which the point of maximum thickness was moved closer to the 40 per cent chord line and the curvatures of the top and bottom surfaces were made more similar. The new wing could be made deeper than that of the Spitfire without risking encounters with compressibility or increasing drag, and was designed with compound straight taper so that chord and thickness near mid-span would be adequate for the installation of a wide-track, inward-retracting undercarriage. The new laminar-flow wing also departed from Spitfire philosophy in featuring dual mainspars.

The fuselage of the Spitfire 21 was to be based on that of the Mark VIII, suitably modified and strengthened to accept the two-stage Griffon 60-series engine. As outlined above, the Mark VIII airframes used to test the fuselage modifications and engine installations proved so successful that the modified aircraft went into production as the Mark XIV. The new wing, however, still promised improvements in warload, weaponry (both the elliptical and laminar-flow designs were intended to accept four 20-mm cannon) and handling. The greater strength of the modified airframe and landing gear—the latter incorporating Seafire lessons—would increase the weight available for weapons and fuel, improving the Spitfire's endurance which by then was regarded as minimal in comparison to more modern aircraft. The taller landing gear would also permit installation of a larger propeller, increasing the speed of the aircraft. Spitfire

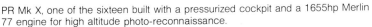
PR Mk X, one of the sixteen built with a pressurized cockpit and a 1655hp Merlin 77 engine for high altitude photo-reconnaissance.

(Imperial War Museum)

21 was ordered in large quantities in mid-1943, preparations being made before the prototype had flown for the construction of 1,500 of the type at Castle Bromwich. The Castle Bromwich aircraft were to have the elliptical wing, but an order placed slightly later in the year with Supermarine was quickly amended to specify the more angular laminar-flow wing.

Fortunately, the 'interim' Marks XIV and XVI were well established in production by the time it was found that the Spitfire 21 with the elliptical wing was a very bug-infested aircraft. Almost a year after the first prototype had flown, and following an extensive series of modifications, the Mark 21 was rejected for service use on account of instability and control difficulties which rendered it generally inferior to the Mark XIV. Substantial modifications followed, and eventually made an acceptable aircraft out of the 21 in time for it to carry out a few patrols over Europe in the closing days of the war. The 120 production aircraft from Castle Bromwich were nearly all delivered post-war.

Meanwhile, the development of the laminar-flow wing had taken a somewhat different course. The new wing was married to a modified, Griffon-powered Spitfire VIII fuselage in mid-1944, but by this time it had been decided to apply the new wing to a completely new fuselage under the name Spiteful. The fuselage was deeper than the Spitfire's, offering a better view for the pilot and more volume for fuel. In order to make use of this space, however, it was necessary to improve the Spiteful's stability when loaded fully aft. The third Spiteful was therefore fitted with a new tail assembly in which the tailplane and elevators were enlarged by means of a 'plug' at the root and the fin was replaced by an altogether new and larger design. Like the tail of the first Spiteful prototypes, this was interchangeable with the Spitfire unit. Another modification introduced by the third Spiteful, the true prototype of the planned Spiteful XIV production aircraft (the choice of the designation has never been fully explained, but may have been a hangover from the original plans to use a fuselage similar to that of the Spitfire XIV), was an engine air intake extended to the nose of the aircraft, resulting in a deeper cowling.

With the end of the war, it was decided that the effort involved in putting the Spiteful into production was unjustified; continuing requirements for piston-engined fighters for close support (and to tide the Royal Air Force and Fleet Air Arm over until jets could take over completely) could be mainly met by cheaper continued production of Spitfires. Additionally, the FAA put its longer-term faith in the radial-engined Sea Fury, less vulnerable to damage of the cooling system than aircraft with liquid-cooled engines. The latter policy stopped development of the Seafang, a navalised Spiteful, although a handful of fixed-wing Seafang 31s and fully navalised 32s were delivered.

Some experimental work with the Spiteful continued, however, and this was to have an impact on the development of the last Spitfires and Seafires. The Seafang was intended from the outset to feature the Griffon 80-series engine, with a modified reduction gear driving contra-rotating propellers. The six-blade Rotol unit finally solved the handling problems caused by propeller torque, and its advantages were clear, especially in the difficult environment of carrier flying. Contra-rotating propellers were also tested on two Spitfire 21s and the single Spiteful XV. The ultimate Spiteful, however, was the XVI; powered by a three-stage-supercharged Griffon 101, the sole Spiteful XVI attained 494 mph (795 km/hr) in level flight during tests in 1947. Only one piston-engined fighter (the Republic XP-47J) can claim a higher speed in a controlled test.

Some of the Spiteful features were fed back into the Spitfire line. In March, 1945, Castle Bromwich started production of the Spitfire 22, differing from the 21 mainly in featuring the all-round-vision hood and cut-down rear fuselage; later aircraft, however, were fitted with the tail unit of the Spiteful, restoring to a great extent the handling qualities which had begun to deteriorate with the Spitfire XIV. The 260 Mark 22s were followed by the slightly heavier, longer-range Mark 24, and 27 of these aircraft were the last to be delivered

from Castle Bromwich before the massive shadow factory reverted entirely to its peacetime role. A further 54 Mark 24s were completed at the Supermarine works at South Marston, and delivery of the last of them in February, 1948 brought production of the Spitfire to a close.

This was not the end of the line for the Supermarine fighter. The Fleet Air Arm had been interested in the Type 356 from its earliest days, and Cunliffe-Owen was tasked early in 1944 with the development of a navalised version of the Spitfire 21. Up to the end of 1945 about 50 of these Seafire 45s were built at Castle Bromwich, but they lacked folding wings and it was discovered that the handling characteristics of the type were not acceptable for carrier operations. Application of contraprops to two Seafire 45s vastly improved the aircraft, and in addition it was found that the stiffer Mark 21-type wing improved gun aiming. The next Seafire variant was the interim FR.46, with contraprops, all-round-vision hood and the Spiteful's fin; a small batch of these aircraft preceded the definitive FR.47 with folding wings, the Spiteful tailplane and—the only member of the whole line to feature the system—fuel injection directly into the cylinders of the Griffon 88 engine. The nose shape of the FR.47 was altered by adoption of the Spiteful's extended air inlet, with the exception of a few early FR.47s which were completed with carburated engines. The last of 90 of the mighty FR.47s left the South Marston line in March, 1949, sharing hardly a single component with the dainty Supermarine 300 of 1936 but still, recognisably, a member of the same family.

The Spitfire and its descendants left their mark on Supermarine, and it could be said that the company rested on its laurels too much, aided by the suddenly slowed pace of development and learning in the British aircraft industry. Supermarine's next aircraft was the Attacker, a competent jet fighter designed in 1944 and using the wing and landing gear of the Spiteful, but by the time the Attacker entered service with the FAA it was outclassed by contemporaries of later design. The Swift, which had started its design life as a swept-wing Attacker, was even less fortunate, being afflicted with stability problems which could not be alleviated in time to avert cancellation of most Swift production. Another long gestation produced the frankly mediocre Scimitar naval fighter, development of which dated back to 1946 but which was almost a contemporary of the Blackburn Buccaneer and McDonnell Phantom when it finally became operational. With the delivery of the last Scimitar in 1960, the name of Supermarine finally vanished from the scene.

The Battle Line

So much has the Spitfire become identified in the lay mind with the Royal Air Force's fighter operations in the 1939-45 war that it is sometimes almost forgotten that the RAF operated other aircraft during that period, or that the Spitfire remained in service, firing its guns in anger, long after 1945 and in many other markings other than RAF roundels. However, it was in the campaign over Southern England in the summer of 1940 that the Spitfire achieved its greatest fame, perhaps because it was the only time that the Spitfire was used in the role for which it was originally designed.

The Spitfire was conceived as an interceptor, with high speed, heavy armament, high rate of climb and the agility to make repeated attacks on its targets as well as to fight off escorting aircraft. It was high level speed and rapid climb which between them shaped the wing of the aircraft, while the modest requirement for range was to affect it throughout its development life and limit its participation in air combat later in the war.

As an element in an air defence system the Spitfire knew few equals even with the appearance of early jet aircraft. In 1940 the Spitfire and Hurricane were incorporated into the world's most effective air defence system, and to explain the success of the aircraft it is necessary to examine this system as a whole, and in particular the technical innovation which had been applied by the RAF to revolutionise the entire concept of air defence. Baldwin's 1930 warning to the citizen that 'there is no power on earth that can protect him from the bomber . . . the bomber will always get through' was based on a simple fact of life. At that time there was no way in which an approaching aircraft or force of aircraft could be detected before it was almost over the territory of the target country. It would then be necessary to scramble aircraft, climb to engage the intruders and identify them before attacking. The air defence structure which had been built up following the raids on London by German aircraft in the 1914-18 war recognised this, leaving a 50-mile 'zone of identification' between the British coast, where the intruders would first be detected, and the 'interception line.' By 1930, increasing speeds of aircraft were inevitably deepening this area to the point where many strategic targets would be vulnerable to air attack before any co-ordinated interception could be made. The bombers would arrive over the target unchallenged in broad daylight: hence Baldwin's pessimism. The most the defences could expect to do would be to harry the attackers as, relieved of their bomb loads, they headed for home. The lumbering RAF bombers of the early 1930s regularly sauntered unscathed past Furies and Bulldogs in the course of exercises.

Radar, developed almost accidentally in the United Kingdom following a search for an electrical 'death ray,' would alter the picture beyond recognition if intelligently used. Fighter Command, formed in 1936 and dedicated primarily to the defence of the United Kingdom, had by 1939 come to rely mainly on radar for the detection and classification of threats, and had integrated it completely into its command structure. The entire air battle was to be conducted from underground command centres fed by radar, with secondary inputs from human observers and commands being issued to the operational groups by telephone.

It was within this system that the Spitfire was to make its vital contribution. At the time of the Munich crisis of September, 1938, the monoplane strength of Fighter Command comprised two squadrons of Hurricanes, but the Spitfire began to join the front line from the following month. It was only in mid-1940, however, that production difficulties with the Spitfire were overcome to the point where the production rate was half that of the simpler Hurricane; the massive Castle Bromwich plant did not begin to open up to its full production rate with the Spitfire II until the second half of the year. It is a comment on the state of German reconnaissance and intelligence that the Woolston factory, the sole source of the only British fighter which could effectively challenge the best of the German fighters, was not attacked until late September, 1940.

Appropriately enough, the Spitfire's first combat encounter was with another new and highly successful type, when a group of Spitfire Is from 603 Squadron attacked a formation of the new Junkers Ju88A-1s, then on final service tests with KG30. Two of the unescorted German bombers were shot down. The Spitfire's combat career in 1939-40 was affected by the insistence of Sir Hugh Dowding, Commander-in-Chief of Fighter Command, that none of the Supermarine fighters should be sent to join the Allied Air Expeditionary Force in France. The only Spitfires to be based in France were a few Spitfire C photo-reconnaissance aircraft of 212 Squadron, which were briefly based near Paris in the spring of 1940. At least one of these aircraft appears to have

Patrol of three Spitfire F.Mk Is, Sqn 19. Spring, 1940.

(Imperial War Museum)

fallen into German hands during the collapse of France. Otherwise, the only Spitfires to land in France were the 92 Squadron aircraft which escorted Winston Churchill's Flamingo transport to Paris in May, 1940, the occasion of the last British refusal to spare the Supermarine fighters for the defence of France.

With the start of the Battle of Britain, the Spitfire came up for the first time against Professor Willy Messerschmitt's Bf 109. Seldom have two aircraft been so equally matched, the advantage switching from one to another according to the manner of combat and the place of action. The Bf 109 and Spitfire represented extreme contrasts in design and philosophy; the wing of the German fighter was nearly 30 per cent smaller than that of the Spitfire, while the capacity of its similarly rated engine was 25 per cent greater. Faster to accelerate in a dive than the Spitfire, and slightly faster in level flight, it became progressively less manoeuvrable than the British fighter as the combat speed was reduced, and at low speeds the bigger-winged Spitfire could roll faster than the Bf 109E, the standard service version of the German fighter during the battle. The Bf 109E was definitely superior to the Spitfire I above 20,000 ft (6,100 m); a considerable part of the credit for this must be laid at the door of Daimler-Benz, who had fitted the German fighter's DB601 engine with an infinitely variable hydraulic transmission to drive the supercharger. The DB601 was unaffected by the drop in output which afflicted the early single-speed Merlin above 'rated altitude'—a concept about which the German pilot did not have to worry.

Two other important features distinguished the adversaries. The Bf 109 was armed with cannon, either two in the wings on the E-4 or one between the cylinder banks of the engine on the E-3, while the 1940 Spitfire was confined to rifle-calibre machine-guns—as mentioned earlier, the service trials of the cannon-armed IB in 1940 were successful only inasmuch as they demonstrated conclusively that the installation was not ready for service use. Experience in the Battle of Britain, however, showed also that the eight-gun armament was not enough to ensure lethality against a target such as the Heinkel He111 bomber, with its self-sealing fuel tanks and 600 lb (272 kg) of armour.

The other major technical difference between the two types lay, like the supercharger drive, in the engine. In developing the DB601 from the basic DB600, Daimler-Benz had installed a system of direct fuel injection into the cylinders. The pilot of the Bf 109, attacked from the rear, could simply push forward on the stick and dive away at full power. A Merlin-powered aircraft treated similarly would suffer an immediate engine cut as the transient negative G force prevented fuel droplets from reaching the engine through the vertically-mounted carburettor. Rolls-Royce had deliberately refrained from using fuel injection in its engines, on the grounds that the fuel from the carburettor, evaporating downstream of the supercharger, cooled the charge entering the cylinder and produced an effect similar to a higher octane rating or higher supercharger boost rating. Neither had the negative-G cut-out been anticipated. Eventually carburetor modifications alleviated the problem, and the last of the whole line—the Seafire FR.47—had fuel injection, but not

before the negative-G cut had provided the Bf 109 with a useful means of escape.

In the opening stages of the Battle of Britain, the Bf 109-equipped *Jagdgeschwader* adopted tactics which best exploited the attributes of their aircraft, providing top cover for the bomber formations above the British fighters' best altitude and engaging British fighter formations when conditions were most favourable. This 'free-chasing' tactic also involved the sort of combat at which the Bf 109 excelled: high-speed diving attacks, a single firing pass with the highly destructive armament and a dive away. The Luftwaffe was moreover adopting a far better combat formation than the British squadrons' three-aircraft 'vics'; the German fighters flew in a loose *Schwarm* of four aircraft, fighting in a *Rotte* of two. Each pilot could scan the sky beyond his companion so that formation flying did not impede the scan for the enemy, and the responsibility was cleanly split between the offensive leader and the defensive wingman. In the early stages of the Battle this formation was adopted by some Fighter Command units.   However, it was still difficult for the British fighters to meet the free-chasing Bf 109s on anything like equal terms. In late July, Bf 109s were first reported to be using the pushover-and-dive tactic to escape from pursuit; around the same time, Fighter Command acknowledged that the Hurricane was outclassed by the German fighter and instituted the policy of using the Hurricanes against the bombers while the Spitfires took on the fighter escort. This was only a partial solution to Fighter Command's loss rate. Fortunately, despite the fact that the Luftwaffe tactics were highly damaging to Fighter Command they were not seen as such by the Luftwaffe *Kampfgeschwader* whose pilots and gunners saw only the apparently unopposed attacks of those British fighters which managed to engage them. A succession of increasingly authoritative orders were transmitted to the *Jagdgeschwader,* requiring them to escort the bombers ever more closely. The fighter leaders understandably protested that this forced them into the slow-speed, medium-level defensive combats, with a great deal of tight turning, where the Spitfire's virtues came to the fore. This was the context of Adolf Galland's much-quoted comment to Hermann Goering, when asked if there was anything he needed for the air battle: 'I should like an outfit of Spitfires for my squadron. Galland certainly did not believe that the Spitfire was intrinsically a superior aircraft to the Bf 109—he would have been a very unusual fighter pilot if he had believed it—but that he appreciated that the performance and characteristics of the British fighter would have been ideal for the job his squadron was now being asked to do.

The reduced effectiveness of the German fighter force, coupled with the deeper penetration and correspondingly shorter combat endurance consequent on the switching of the brunt of the attack to London, gave the British intercepters the chance they needed to attack the main bomber formations with a steadily decreasing degree of interference. The Bf 109s were even assigned to escort the Bf 110 'destroyer' fighters which were themselves intended to provide support for the bomber squadrons but had proved incapable of defending themselves against the RAF fighters. By mid-September the bomber losses had mounted to the point where the daylight campaign was untenable. A minor incident that month marked the end of the Spitfire IB's brief career; eight of the aircraft, on service trials with 19 Squadron, attacked a formation of Bf 110s, no fewer than six of the Spitfires suffering gun stoppages almost immediately. The Spitfire squadron subsequently exchanged its IBs for a scratch team of IAs drawn from maintenance units.

Late September and early October, however, brought a new problem. Now that the Luftwaffe bomber squadrons were raiding by night without fighter escort, the Bf 109 units were left free to conduct nuisance bombing raids, generally releasing their single bombs from high altitude before the population of the attacked area could be alerted. The Spitfires sent up to intercept these high-flying intruders, which were now unencumbered by bombers, found themselves at a serious disadvantage, but the raids were eventually stopped by a combination of worsening weather, increasing Fighter Command strength and the introduction of the Spitfire II and Hurricane II, with much improved high-altitude performance.

By the end of 1940 the Photographic Development Unit (PDU) was well established, and was relying almost entirely on Spitfire conversions. The PDU was unusual in that it owed its beginnings to an ostensibly civilian operation, headed by Sidney Cotton, which before the war had operated an apparently innocent Lockheed transport around Europe. In fact the Lockheed was equipped with long-focal-length cameras in a concealed installation, and the lessons learned about heated lenses and other necessary items of equipment were applied in the conversion of Spitfire Is to photo-reconnaissance aircraft. Between July and December of 1940 the PDU carried out 841 sorties over German-occupied areas, losing ten aircraft.

The work of the PDU—later renamed the Photographic Reconnaissance unit or PRU—became increasingly important as the RAF bombing campaign against Germany intensified, but some of its most valuable and hazardous early work involved the investigation of new systems being put into service by the German forces. In the first two months of 1941 PRU Spitfires revealed the shape of the Freya early warning radar, allowing its performance and characteristics

to be assessed. In this area, one of the greatest strengths of the PRU was the ability of successively improved reconnaissance Spitfires to maintain *routine* surveillance of important sites, so that British Intelligence would be immediately alerted to any development by changes in the picture. An advantage of the Spitfire in this role was that it was a dual-purpose aircraft; as well as carrying long-focus cameras at high level the PR Spitfires could be fitted with an oblique camera facing to port for low-level 'Dicer' sorties, which were highly dangerous but justified when the reward was a detailed photograph of a new electronic installation.

A more aggressive role was taken by the Spitfire squadrons—by now including an increasing proportion of the much improved Spitfire V—in the 'fighter sweeps' which the RAF conducted against German fighter forces in Northern Europe in 1941. A small force of bombers was used as bait to draw the Luftwaffe into combat with a massive fighter escort divided into a close escort, escort cover groups and free-chasing target-support wings. However, the introduction of the Spitfire V yielded less of a combat advantage than had been expected, because its service entry coincided with that of the aerodynamically refined Bf 109F and only just preceded that of the Focke-Wulf Fw190, an aircraft of later design that outclassed and outperformed the Spitfire V in every operational characteristic except turning circle. Development and introduction into service of the Spitfire IX was not in time to prevent the Luftwaffe from achieving local air superiority over the Channel during the escape of the warships *Scharnhorst, Gneisenau* and *Prinz Eugen* from Brest to Wilhelmshaven and Kiel in February, 1942; nor was the improved type available in sufficient numbers to prevent heavy RAF losses (amounting to 106 aircraft) in the air operations supporting the abortive Dieppe raid in August of that year. This was also the period of the first high-speed hit-and-run raids by German fighter-bombers on British targets, and only with the introduction of the Spitfire XII could the British fighter effectively counter these low-level intruders.

The year of 1942 was the first in which the Spitfire was deployed in any numbers outside the United Kingdom. Following the entry of the Soviet Union into the war, 143 Spitfire Vs (some converted from earlier Marks) were deliv-

Spitfire F. Mk I

Spitfire F. Mk Vc

ered to the Soviet Union. It was the intensifying North Africa campaign, however, which made the greatest demands on the Spitfire force. At that time the Spitfire was still the only Allied fighter available in any quantities which could meet contemporary German combat aircraft on equal terms, and the deployment of a force of Spitfires into the Mediterranean theatre became a high priority. The problem was that the strengthened Luftwaffe forces in Sicily were a well-nigh impenetrable obstacle to the shipment of Spitfires to Malta—the unsinkable aircraft carrier around which the air strategy in the Mediterranean revolved—while the Spitfire apparently lacked the range to be ferried by air from the nearest secure base at Gibraltar. Starting in March, 1942, therefore, standard Spitfire Vs modified by the addition of a non-jettisonable ventral fuel tank were carried to a point off the Algerian coast by aircraft carriers and launched to fly the remaining 660 miles (1,060 km) to Malta. Between March and October, 367 Spitfires were safely delivered to Malta in this way, and as the campaign developed the fighters were transferred from Malta to North African bases. Special procedures were developed to get the overloaded Spitfires, manned by land-based pilots making their first carrier take-offs, safely into the air. Later in the year, Spitfires fitted with 170 gal (770 lit) drop tanks were ferried non-stop to Malta from Gibraltar; the aircraft were also fitted with 29 gal (132 lit) auxiliary oil tanks similar to that installed in the modified nose of long-range reconnaissance Spitfires, which replaced the usual tropical filter. (The ungainly tropical air filter installed on Mediterranean Spitfires and early Seafires was later replaced with a more discreet and streamlined design.) Non-stop ferrying from Gibraltar would have become the standard method of delivering Spitfires to the Mediterranean theatre in 1943, but the collapse of the German forces in North Africa after El Alamein eliminated the need for such expedients.

October, 1942, also saw the operational debut of the Seafire in support of the Allied invasion of French North Africa, the type being blooded in action in the following month against Dewoitine D.520 fighters of the Vichy French forces. The Seafire's first kill, in fact, was an American-built Martin 167 light bomber of the Vichy forces. Seafires were

not the only Supermarine fighters used in support of the Operation Torch landings; Spitfire VBs of the US Army Air Force 31st and 52nd Fighter Groups also took part in the action. The USAAF Spitfire groups stemmed from the Eagle squadrons which, manned by American volunteers, had supported the RAF in the Battle of Britain, and the Supermarine fighter was used on a larger scale by the US units based in the United Kingdom. (The only US fighters available in quantity before the end of 1942 were the mediocre Curtiss P-40 and Bell P-39.) Before the North African invasion the USAAF Spitfires had participated in some RAF fighter sweeps and had also provided escorts for early short-range daylight bombing missions. After the USAAF fighter force had converted to newer American fighters the 8th Air Force continued to use a few of the photo-reconnaissance versions in Europe.

Both in North Africa and in Europe the Spitfire encountered a new threat in 1942, taking the ungainly shape of the Junkers Ju86. This pre-war German bomber/transport had been retired from the front-line bomber squadrons before the Battle of Britain, but had been made the subject of development work aimed at producing a high-altitude bomber and reconnaissance aircraft. In May, 1942, the first version of this aircraft, the Ju86P, commenced operations from Crete over Cairo and Alexandria, photographing defence preparations and military installations with impunity. It was a stripped-down Spitfire V which carried out the first successful interception of the high-flying but unprotected Junkers, bringing the reconnaissance aircraft down with the mighty armament of two 0.5 in (12.7 mm) machine guns.

By the time the Junkers Ju86 was used for resumed flights over Britain, however, the aircraft had undergone some changes. The most obvious of these was a further massive extension of the wingspan, but the two Ju86Rs deployed to Northern France in August, 1942, were modified to carry a single 550 lb (250 kg) bomb. The extra span and engine modifications of the Ju86R put it outside the reach of the Spitfire V, and even the high-altitude, pressurised Mark VI was, due to its single-stage Merlin, incapable of intercepting the new aircraft. The Mark VII with two-stage Merlin and pressure cabin was not yet ready, and the German bombers were able to raid British targets unopposed. Air raid warnings

Spitfire F. Mk IX (left)

(Imperial War Museum)

Spitfire F. Mk IXc

(Imperial War Museum)

1 Seat
2 Control column
3 Heel board
4 Rudder pedal adjusting wheel
5 Rudder pedal
6 Radiation flap control lever
7 Map case
8 Oil dilution pushbotton
9 Rudder trimming tab handwheel
10 Pressure head heater switch
11 Elevator trimming tab handwheel
12 Bomb switch
13 Crowbar
14 Door catch
15 Camera indication supply plug
16 Mixture lever
17 Throttle lever
18 Propeller control lever
19 Boost control cut-out
20 Radio controller
21 Ignition switch
22 Brake triple pressure gauge
23 Clock
24 Elevator tabs position indicator
25 Oxygen regulator
26 Navigation lights switch
27 Flap control
28 Airspeed indicator
29 Altimeter
30 Gun and cannon three-position
   pushbutton (Spitfire Vb)
31 Cockpit light switches
32 Direction indicator and setting nob
33 Artificial horizon
34 Reflector gun sight, type GM-2
35 Rear view mirror
36 Ventilator control
37 Rate of climb indicator
38 Turning indicator
39 Booster coil pushbutton
40 Engine starting pushbutton
41 Oil pressure gauge
42 Oil temperature gauge
43 Fuel contents gauge and pushbutton
44 Radiator temperature gauge
45 Boost pressure gauge
46 Fuel pressure warning lamp
47 Engine speed indicator
48 Ventilator control
49 Stowage for reflector sight lamp

50 Cockpit light
51 Signalling switchbox
52 Remote contactor and switch
53 Fuel tank pressurising cock control
54 Slow running cut-out control
55 Priming pump
56 Fuel cock
57 Compass
58 Undercarriage control lever
59 Harness release
60 Oxygen hose
61 I.F.F. controls
62 CO_2 cylinder for undercarriage emergency
   system
63 Oxygen supply cock
64 Windscreen de-icing pump
65 Windscreen de-icing needle valve
66 Undercarriage emergency lowering control
67 Windscreen de-icing cock

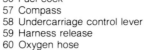

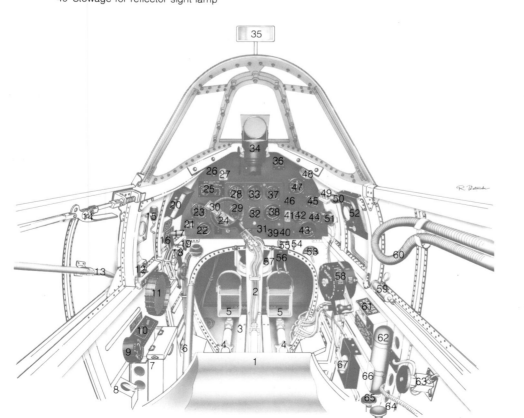

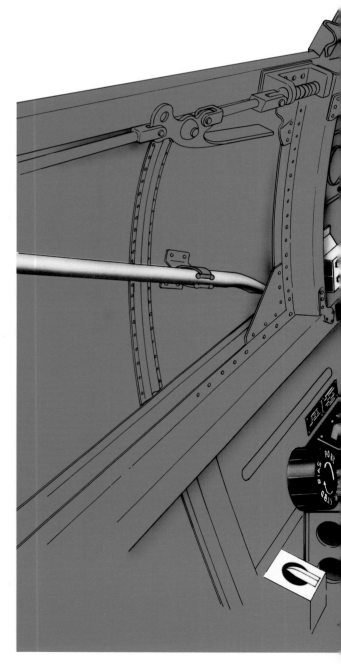

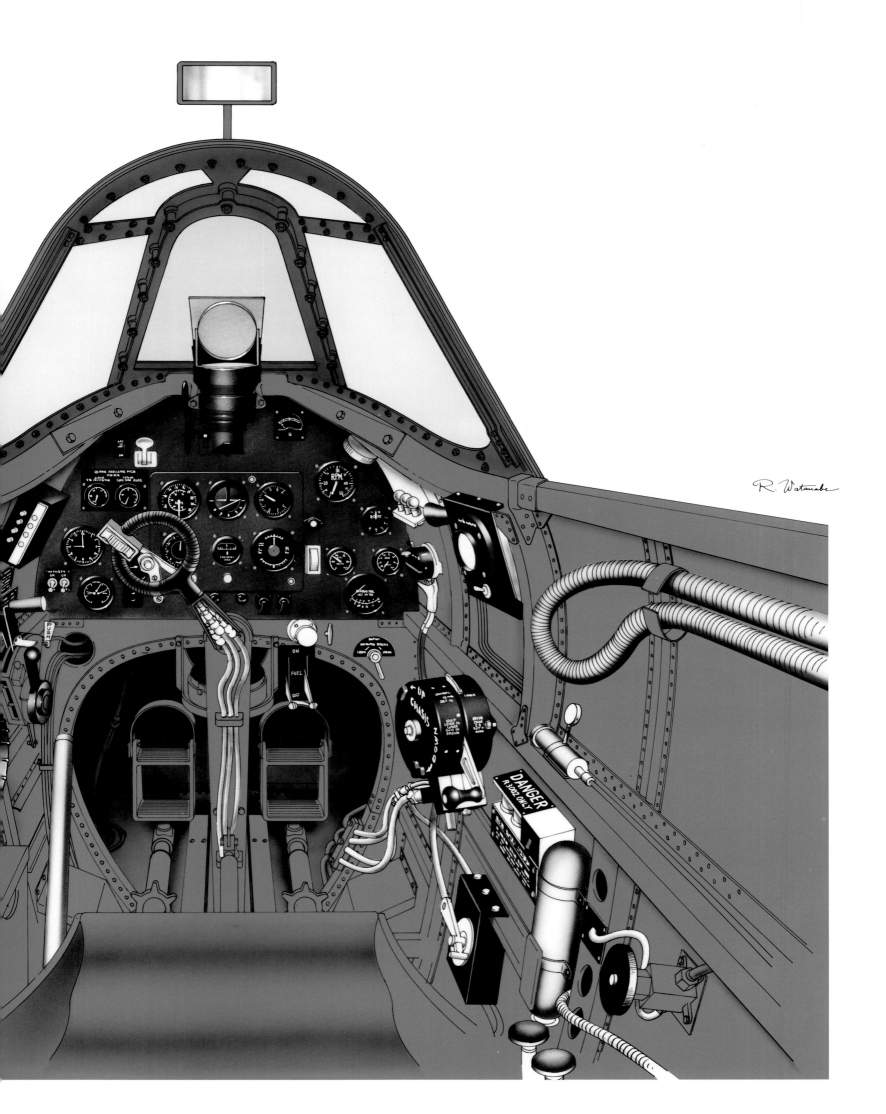

R. Watanabe

were not sounded for single intruders, with the result that on August 28 a single bomb from a Ju86R killed 48 people at Bristol. After this incident, a special unit was formed at Northolt, flying Spitfire IXs modified by removal of the machine guns, armour and other equipment and fitted with a lightweight wooden propeller. Medically selected pilots were trained to fly at high altitudes without pressurisation. On September 12 one of the modified aircraft put a cannon shell through one of the intruders at 44,000 ft (13,400 m), and although the Ju86R regained its base operations over Britain were halted.

With the increasing tempo of Spitfire production and the availability of newer fighters in the European theatre, the Spitfire began to spread its wings more widely in 1943. Early in the year 54 Squadron took its Spitfire Vs to Darwin to protect the Australian mainland from the Japanese air forces. In August the Portuguese air force, which had ordered a batch of Spitfire Is before war broke out, finally took delivery of 15 of the type; these rather elderly aircraft were supplemented soon after by Spitfire Vs. One unit which had an eventful year was 155 Squadron, which took its new Mark VIIIs (including some unusual four-cannon aircraft) to the Soviet Union before joining a rapidly expanding Spitfire force in Burma late in 1943. Operations in the Far East brought the Spitfire up against the Japanese Navy and Army fighters, of which the foremost was the redoubtable Mitsubishi A6M Zero-Sen. The A6M was an unusual opponent for the Spitfire, in that the British fighter enjoyed superiority in the areas where it was inferior to its other contemporaries, and vice versa. For example, it was faster in level and diving flight than the A6M, but the Japanese fighter could turn inside it at low speeds, and the tactics adopted against the A6M by the Spitfire tended to be the reverse of those used against its other adversaries.

September, 1943, saw the first extensive combat use of the Seafire. The decision to invade Italy at the 'knee' rather than fighting all the way up from Sicily created problems in providing air cover over the invasion beaches, because the selected invasion site at Salerno was too far from the Allied air bases in Sicily for effective air cover to be maintained. Accordingly it was decided to provide air support for the operation from a force of Royal Navy carriers equipped mainly with Seafire IICs and LIICs. The Seafires brought down few of the German and Italian aircraft, partly because the tactics used were predominantly defensive and many of the raiders were bomb-carrying *Jabo* Bf 109s and Fw190s. But in 713 sorties, no fewer than 42 of the 120 Seafires involved had been lost or written off, including 32 wrecked in landing accidents, while 39 more of the fighters had been damaged in deck accidents. Although the operation served its purpose of providing air cover until the land forces could provide secure airstrips, the Seafire force had virtually ceased to exist by Salerno D-day plus 3. The bad experience of Salerno not unnaturally coloured the Navy's subsequent view of the Seafire; although development of a Seafire version with a stronger undercarriage was initiated shortly after the Salerno operations, it was to be another three years before this aircraft, the Seafire 17, entered service. Meanwhile, deliveries of purpose-built American carrier fighters to the Fleet Air Arm were picking up speed, and the Seafire suf-

fered by comparison.

The Spitfire, however, continued to be one of the mainstays of Fighter Command as the invasion of Europe approached. In 1943 the Mark XII had joined the home-defence force to help counter the threat of 'tip-and-run' attacks by German fighter-bombers, and at the beginning of the following year the Spitfire XIV appeared, keeping the Spitfire well in the front line despite the delayed appearance of the Mark 21. The US daylight bombing offensive was by this time drawing away an increasing proportion of the German fighter force in Western Europe, and the Royal Air Force found itself concentrating on low-level fighter sweeps and ground-attack operations. The steady re-equipment of the squadrons with Mark IXs from Castle Bromwich or the new Mark XIVs, both with the ability to carry unguided rockets or bombs, helped this trend; the remaining Mark Vs were also converted in 1943 to a low-altitude configuration.

Tactics of close support developed in the Western Desert and Italy were naturally developed and improved in the campaign in Northern France. The lesson learned in the early stages of the Desert campaign was that close co-operation was essential at all levels if the Army and Air Force were to work together. Air Marshal Harry Broadhurst, supporting British forces in Europe in command of 83 Group, moved his headquarters alongside that of the commander of the army group he was supporting. At the air force bases, Army liaison officers kept the squadrons informed about what was going on in the ground battle, while at the front operations were controlled by RAF personnel in radio-equipped vehicles. Another part of this system was the fighter-reconnaissance aircraft, a low-level fighter with a specially trained pilot and an oblique camera; the FR Spitfires not only reported on enemy movements but provided the British commanders with exact and up-to-date information on the positions of their own forces. The fighter pilots' tallies of 'kills' were expanded to include enemy vehicles; the Spitfire, however, was less suitable for attacks against armoured vehicles or locomotives than the more heavily armed Typhoon and Tempest.

The Spitfire played an important part in the fight against the German 'revenge weapons' on which Hitler had ordered a tremendous development effort in the belief that there was no effective defence against them. In the case of the Fieseler Fi103 or V-1 flying bomb this was certainly not true, because the missile's straight flightpath made it a relatively easy target and its speed was not quite sufficient to ensure its escape from the latest fighter aircraft. Spitfire XIVs and Tempest Vs were the only fighters with enough speed to catch the V-1s—either overhauling them and toppling the relatively cheap and crude guidance system with their wingtip vortices or blasting the bomb at perilously close range with cannon—until the first RAF Meteor jet fighters entered service. The Fi103 could thus be countered by conventional means; not so the A-4 or V-2, a ballistic missile which presented an impossible target once it was off the ground. After heavy bombers had wrecked the massive concrete bunkers from which the rockets were originally to have been launched, the German Army switched to small, mobile launch teams carrying their missiles on the Meilerwagen transporter/erector. The search for these sites, well hidden and inevitably protected by heavy flak, was a difficult task; bomb-carrying Spitfires attacked the sites to some effect, but the missile firings on London only ceased when the front line was pushed out of range. Firings at Antwerp and Rotterdam, however, continued until the end of the war. Some of the armed reconnaissance patrols over suspected A-4 sites towards the end of the war involved Spitfire 21s, one squadron of which became operational before the end of the war in Europe.

Meanwhile, the first Seafires had been heading for the Far East. By now the Fleet Air Arm had largely re-equipped with Seafire IIIs and LIIIs, the folding wings of the new type facilitating carrier operations and allowing more aircraft to be carried. By this time it was accepted that the high climb speed and rapid acceleration of the Seafire, which was superior to the American fighters in these respects, suited it mainly to the defence of the fleet against air attack; and by early 1945, when the first Seafire units were engaged in support of carrier-aircraft strikes against oil refineries in the East Indies, suicide tactics were increasingly being used by the Japanese Army Air Force. In normal air-to-air combat, however, the fighters employed in South-East Asia by the Japanese were outclassed by the Seafire. In March, 1945, Seafires became operational with the carriers of the British Pacific Fleet in time for the invasion of Okinawa, in which the Supermarine fighter again filled its role of protecting the carriers against Kamikaze suicide attacks. Only in the last days of the war were the Seafires used on ground attacks against Japanese air bases.

The post-war run-down of the British Spitfire force was rapid. The Merlin-engined variants went first, being replaced by Griffon-powered aircraft built towards the end of the war or shortly afterwards and held in storage. Spitfire IXs based in Palestine, for example, were replaced with Mark 18s (Arabic numerals replacing Roman shortly after the war) and the Spitfire 22 re-equipped many of the Auxiliary Air Force squadrons until these received jets in 1950-51. The RAF fighter force had not fought its last combat with the end of the 1939-45 war, however. In 1948, the RAF Spitfires of 32 Squadron, based at Ramat David in Palestine, were attacked by Egyptian Mark IXs, apparently mistaking them for Spitfires acquired by the Israeli Air Force. The second wave of four attacking aircraft failed to escape before they were pursued and easily overhauled by the faster Mark 18s of 208 Squadron, which destroyed them without further loss.

Mark 18s also saw action in Malaya, being used for cannon and rocket strikes against suspected guerilla hideouts. The effectiveness of such tactics was doubtful due to the lack of precise information as to where the hideouts were, and later the RAF switched to using more heavily armed aircraft such as Bristol Brigands (which also had a much longer loiter endurance than the Spitfire) and even carpet-bombed suspected areas with Lincolns. The last RAF fighter unit to use the Spitfire was No 80 Squadron, which operated its Mark 24s from Kai Tak airfield at Hong Kong until January 1952.

With the Royal Navy, the Seafire enjoyed increased importance when the Lend-Lease Corsairs and

Hellcats were returned to the United States after the end of the war. The new Griffon-powered Seafire XV replaced the Merlin-engined versions by mid-1946, at least as far as front-line units were concerned; between that time and mid-1947, however, operations with these aircraft were severely restricted after a succession of accidents caused by a faulty design feature in the supercharger clutch. This was remedied in time for the improved Seafire 17—with its stronger landing gear—to be issued to front-line units and the newly formed Royal Naval Volunteer Reserve squadrons. It was an RNVR squadron which took delivery of the first Seafire FR.46s, more advanced than the contemporary front-line Seafire but lacking folding wings, in July, 1948. The definitive FR.47 embarked later in that year aboard HMS Triumph, and arrived in Singapore in September, 1949; in the following month the ultimate descendant of the Supermarine 300 fired ordonance in anger for the first time, carrying out rocket strikes against guerilla bases in Malaya. With the outbreak of war in Korea, Triumph took the Seafires to the Yellow Sea, where the fighters carried out strafing, ground attack and air defence missions until normal attrition forced the retirement of the carrier and its few remaining aircraft. The disembarkation of Triumph's last Seafires in November 1950 marked the end of the type's career with the Royal Navy's first-line units, the last RNVR and training units retiring their Mark 17s and FR.47s in 1954.

The year 1954 saw the replacement of the last strategic reconnaissance Spitfire PR.19s in Royal Air Force service, the last of this variant soldiering on for meteorological reconnaissance until 1957, when the last aircraft of the type was retired from British service. By this time the Spitfire had also come to the end of its career under foreign flags, a career which might be said to have started with the pre-war Portuguese order for 12 Spitfire Is. Eventually, Portugal took delivery of Spitfire Is in August, 1943, these aircraft being retired in 1948; the more modern Spitfire VBs delivered in the same year as the older aircraft were retired in 1952. The Portuguese Spitfires were noteworthy in that they were the only aircraft of the type to operate outside Allied command during the 1939-45 war.

Post-war reconstruction of European air forces was helped in some instances by the pilots who had flown with the wartime RAF while in exile from their occupied homelands. Norway, Denmark and Greece all took delivery of surplus Mark IXs in 1947; the first two also received a trio of PR.XIs each, while Greece became the only export customer for the Mark XVI. Some Spitfires reached Eastern Europe, serving briefly in Yugoslavia; another group of Mark IXs was supplied to Italy. The Royal Dutch Air Force was one of two European air forces to use the Supermarine fighter in combat, employing its clipped-wing Mark IXs against insurgents in Indonesia before that country's independence.

The other European air arm to use the type in anger was the French Aeronavale, which took delivery of 48 refurbished Seafire LIIIs in March 1946. The Seafires departed for France's South-East Asian possessions abroad Arromanches in October 1948, and a few air strikes were carried out against Viet Minh insurgents late in that year. Landing accidents were common, as they had been with the Royal Navy's

Seafires and by early 1949 *Arromanches* has so few service-able aircraft that there was no longer any point keeping the ship in the Vietnam area. The Seafires were replaced by equally elderly but more reliable Grumman F6F Hellcats in 1950.

Seafires were also exported to Canada, two squadrons of Royal Canadian Navy Seafire XVs being formed in 1945. They were replaced by Hawker Sea Furies in mid-1948. The last Seafires to see combat, however, were probably a batch of 20 Seafire XVs delivered to Burma for counter-insurgency operations in 1951. These aircraft had been extensively modified by the installation of non-folding Spitfire 18 wings and the removal of carrier equipment, and were thus very similar to the Spitfire 18s also operated by the Union of Burma Air Force, the main difference between the two types being the Seafires' single-stage Griffon engines and the Spitfires' all-round-vision hoods. The Seafire also took off its seaboots for the Irish Air Corps, which took delivery of 12 denavalised Seafire IIIs in 1947; the same air force was one of two purchasers for the two-seat Spitfire T.IX, converted from the standard aircraft by the installation of a second, separate cockpit behind and above the first.

A major Spitfire operator in Europe was the Royal Swedish Air Force, which acquired 50 unused surplus Spitfire PR.19s from the United Kingdom in 1948. Designated S31 in Swedish service, the aircraft were operated by the F11 wing based at Nykoping until they were superseded by more modern jet aircraft in August 1955. The biggest Spitfire operator other than the RAF, however, was the Royal Indian Air Force (as it was named between 1945 and 1948) which took delivery of 250 Spitfire VIIIs towards the end of the 1939-45 war. From 1945 these aircraft were supplemented by Griffon-powered Mark XIVs, and in 1947 the Indian Air Force gained a conversion-training capability with the delivery of half-a-dozen two-seater T.IXs. Four years later, India acquired from British stocks a squadron of Mark 18s and a squadron of PR.19s, these being the last Spitfires delivered from the UK. India's last Spitfires were retired in 1955.

Egypt and Syria also took delivery of Spitfires, the former receiving Mark 22s to replace its Mark IXs in 1950, and as far as the British were concerned these were the last Spitfires to be delivered to the Middle East. The State of Israel had other ideas, and despite an arms embargo the emerging Israeli air force managed to conclude a contract with dollar-hungry Czechoslovakia for the supply of 50 Spitfire LF.IX fighters, as these were being replaced at that time by Soviet aircraft. The Spitfires were preceded into service by Avia C-210s—developments of the Bf 109—with the result that Spitfires and Messerschmitts were to find themselves fighting side by side against Egyptian Spitfires.

The first C-210s had been ferried to Israel abroad Douglas C-54s acquired in the USA, but in 1948 the French closed the airport of Ajaccio to the transports and the air route to Zatec in Czechoslovakia was blocked. An attempt to fly the Spitfires non-stop from Zatec to Ramat David in Israel succeeded only in part, two out of the five Spitfires in the formation being forced to land at Rhodes. Eventually, however, 50 Spitfires reached Israel from Czechoslovakia, proving very much more popular than the unwieldy Junkers-powered Avia. In early 1949, Israeli Spitfire IXs shot down a number of RAF Spitfire 18s based in the Canal Zone when the British fighters were carrying out reconnaissance missions over Israeli-held territory to check compliance with the ceasefire which had ended the 1948 war: thus, the last RAF Spitfires to be destroyed in fighter-versus-fighter combat were shot down by Spitfires, just as their last victims had been Spitfires.

The Israeli Air Force acquired 35 more Spitfires HF.IXEs from Italy in 1950-51, and these aircraft replaced the Avia fighters. In 1954, however, Israel acquired Gloster Meteor jet fighters and the Spitfires were retired. Thirty of the newer aircraft were sold to Burma, but once again there was a problem of delivery because Arab states would refuse landing and refuelling rights to any aircraft originating in Israel. An attempt to deliver the aircraft via Sicily, complete with false flight plans alleging that they originated in Britain, was unsuccessful, and the aircraft had to be refitted with long-range fuel tanks and delivered by a northerly route. These reconditioned Spitfire IXs joined the motley Burmese force of Mark 18s and denavalised Seafire XVs, operating against insurgents in Burma into the late 1950s. By 1956, only these aircraft and a few RAF meteorological reconnaissance PR.19s remained in service out of the 22,000 Spitfires and Seafires built, and by the end of 1957 the aircraft passed into history.

A number of Spitfires, however, have remained in flying condition, preserved by the RAF, by groups of enthusiasts or by wealthy individuals. In the making of the film *The Battle of Britain* in 1968, a force of 12 airworthy Spitfires was assembled, including one Spitfire II which had actually participated in the 1940 conflict. Some of these still fly, and have actually been joined in the air recently by newly restored aircraft; such is the appeal and fascination of the Spitfire that the last of the type seem set to continue flying indefinitely.

(Imperial War Museum)